Your First Restaurant - An Essential Guide

Your First Restaurant - An Essential Guide

How to plan, research, analyze, finance, open, and operate your own wildly successful eatery.

Daniel Boardman

ISBN: 0692810455
ISBN 13: 9780692810453
Library of Congress Control Number: 2016919591
Edith Street Publications, Albuquerque, NEW MEXICO

Table of Contents

Introduction

WHY SHOULD YOU OPEN A RESTAURANT?

In my varied and meandering professional life, one of the most fulfilling things I have ever done has been to plan, open, and run restaurants. Each one is nicely profitable, and my capable managers limit the amount of my time required for any one location. The emotional rewards are enormous. Being a part of a committed, diligent team that works ceaselessly to please customers is rewarding. So is hearing the din and chatter of a dining room full of happy patrons and seeing mountains of plates come back scraped clean. Watching the realization of concepts that began as fanciful ideas and have grown into vibrant and thriving restaurants never fails to touch me and spark a profound sense of gratitude.

A WORD OF CAUTION

Of course, the restaurant game is fun only as long as your restaurant is profitable. A restaurant failure can be financially and emotionally devastating. Since I have opened and grown my restaurants, and in the same and similar neighborhoods, I have watched a handful of other restaurants open and fail within a year, or open and struggle and never quite reach a point of thriving profitability.

Why do so many new restaurants fail while others around them thrive? There is no shortage of widely differing opinions as to the causes of restaurant failure and, in this book, I offer an entire chapter on the subject.

But if I had to identify only one overarching reason for underperformance and failure of new restaurants, I would point to the pervasiveness of faulty restaurant business-related decision-making. Those new to the restaurant industry, understandably, often lack the tool chest of analytical decision-making tools; the frameworks and matrices required for them to most effectively navigate the perpetual storm of often conflicting, misleading, and missing information, and to plot a course that will lead them to making decisions that will yield the best outcomes in any situation.

WHAT THIS BOOK CAN DO FOR YOU

With this book, I hope to remedy that. If you are contemplating opening your first restaurant, I want to arm you with the knowledge base and the logical, analytical, real-world restaurant decision-making skill set that will help you avoid disastrous financial wrong turns and that will dramatically increase your odds and speed of success. I hope this effort helps you to create a highly successful restaurant, one that delights your customers; provides meaningful jobs for your staff; and is financially, emotionally, and creatively rewarding for you.

HOW I BECAME A RESTAURATEUR

In 2010, as the national real estate market ground to a standstill, I saw my two primary sources of income – brokering commercial real estate and teaching commercial real estate investment analysis nationally – evaporate. In my early 50s, with time on my hands, but only a humble amount of capital and no meaningful food industry experience, I decided to open a restaurant.

For me this was not a lifelong dream. One day I happened to walk by a down-at-the-heels, struggling drive-through taco stand a few blocks from my house and began reflecting on its business, or lack thereof. It hit me how out-of-step the business was with its context: a turn-of-the-century neighborhood that had been gentrified over the last 20 years. The restaurant was located near the gateway to downtown and its sizeable workforce, and was on the side of the street on which people headed to work travel, yet it didn't even open until long after the morning rush hour subsided. What if someone were to give the building a cosmetic facelift to make its appearance more harmonious with the neighborhood? What if the business were rebranded, opened early every morning, and sold high-quality breakfast burritos and espresso drinks and maybe simple but thoughtful boxed lunches for customers to grab on their way to work?

I sought out the owner and expressed my interest in buying the business. No response. I tried a second time. After my third failed attempt, I decided to investigate other possible locations for my nascent restaurant concept.

I found several drive-through restaurant locations available, but none impressed me. Eventually, an odd building caught my eye. It housed not a restaurant, but a maid service. However, it did have abundant parking, and its zoning allowed a restaurant with a drive-through window.

The surrounding area, though, gave me pause. The site sat at the convergence of four separate neighborhoods, each with very different populations. To the north was a vacant and derelict shopping center; to the east, an area dominated by lower-income apartment renters; to the west, a neighborhood of well-kept, older, owner-occupied single-family homes and relatively high household incomes; and to the south, a hospital, a medical center, and an air force base with 23,000 employees. I wondered: could any one restaurant concept appeal to enough people from such diverse demographics to win over the critical mass of customers required to sustain it?

Up for a challenge, I purchased the property, hired an architect and contractor, converted the building into a restaurant with a drive-through window and small dining room, and six months later opened a counter-service breakfast and lunch café focused on made-from-scratch traditional

Northern New Mexican-style cuisine. I named it Tia Betty Blue's, which, linguistically, much like the food we serve, reflects a mash-up of local Hispanic and Anglo cultures.

The basic concept proved immediately popular, although there was abundant room for improvement. We spent the first two years making near-daily incremental changes in our menu items and processes, and fine-tuning our concept to better fit our customers. Business grew steadily, and to accommodate it we expanded our seating capacity almost every six months. Now in its fourth year, Tia Betty's is thriving. The restaurant has received numerous local-favorite awards, has a fiercely loyal following, and is viewed by many as a neighborhood institution, a place to take out-of-town visitors, a place where patrons routinely scribble glowing notes of praise about the restaurant on paper napkins and slip them under the glass tabletops, where they become a permanent part of the ambiance.

JUST WAFFLES – A SECOND RESTAURANT

In the spring of 2014 I was approached by the owner of a cute, commercially zoned, 1920s-vintage house, located in a revitalized neighborhood full of trendy bars and hip eateries. The owner offered to remodel the building as necessary to convert it into a restaurant and proposed an interesting lease structure, one based almost entirely on the future restaurant's gross monthly sales. The lease structure sounded great, but the only space available for a commercial kitchen and dishwashing sinks was the original residential kitchen, a closet-sized space of less than 70 square feet. Realizing that there was no way that standard commercial kitchen equipment would fit in this postage-stamp-sized kitchen, I wondered just what sort of equipment would fit. Waffle irons! The concept of La Wafflería – the word waffle with the Spanish suffix "ría" meaning a place that sells that thing – was born. La Wafflería offers a couple dozen imaginative sweet and savory waffle and sauce combinations as well as a "build your own" menu that allows for over 30,000 waffle combinations.

Since its opening La Wafflería has been extremely popular, with weekends marked by long lines, full seating capacity, and relentless demand. After six months we were able to commandeer an adjacent building to house our now much roomier kitchen and to add outdoor seating. La Wafflería continues to grow and has received numerous local favorite awards, has won several "best of" awards, and was recently featured in the Cooking Channel program *Cheap Eats*.

Housed in a nearly 100-year-old residence with a roaring fire in the fireplace, walls decorated with a curated collection of 1930s chrome Art Deco waffle irons, and vintage black and white waffle-themed-images, La Waff has become its own sort of neighborhood institution, popular with university students, young families, and senior citizens and seems to be on many people's "I've got to show you this place!" list.

TACOS AND ICE CREAM – A THIRD RESTAURANT

In late 2015 I became fascinated with the street-style tacos of southern Mexico, particularly the vertical spit cooked al pastor style of taco, and spent a week in Mexico City visiting over 30 different taquerías. This led me to open my third restaurant, El Cotorro, In the summer of 2016. It employs a counter-service concept and features craft tacos and house-made Mexico-City-style ice cream, and is located in a former furniture store less than a block from La Wafflería. Many of the initial customers for El Cotorro have been the regulars at my other restaurants, have become fans of my type of restaurant, my brand, and were excited to try the latest installment.

One

Now is the time: The dawning golden age of independent restaurants

I believe we are entering a new golden age for local, independently-owned restaurants, one fueled by the convergence of a number of unrelated trends – continued growth in the food industry, dramatically shifting consumer preferences, and increasing use of crowd-sourced review sites and social media. In addition, commercial real estate market conditions in many areas of the country favor buyers and tenants over sellers and landlords. The confluence of these conditions is molding a new business landscape, one that is amazingly fertile and hospitable to the success of the independent restaurant. If you are considering opening a restaurant, your timing is excellent.

Americans spend more money on restaurants every year than the year before, and last year total restaurant industry annual sales reached a record high of over $700 billion. As well, the restaurant's slice of the food dollar is growing. That is, the percentage of every dollar that Americans spend on food that goes to restaurants rather than to a grocery store has been steadily increasing and is now at an all-time high, with nearly half of all money spent on food last year being spent on eating out.

The restaurant industry is not just growing; it's changing rapidly. Major shifts in consumer preferences are unfolding, changes in the restaurant goer's preferences and behaviors that have the potential to significantly advantage local independent restaurants at the expense of large multi-state chains.

When it comes to food, Americans are suddenly becoming much more daring. An amazing 64 percent of consumers report that they are more adventurous in their restaurant food choices today than they were just two years ago*, a huge increment of change in a short period of time. This trend may be part of a larger trend of Americans taking greater interest in their food, as evidenced by The Food Channel and similar food-centric media outlets, and it may be enabled by Yelp and similar crowd-sourced restaurant review sites, which serve to reduce the risk of a bad experience when selecting a lesser-known restaurant (more on that later). Whatever the reason, this trend toward adventurous eating clearly benefits local independent restaurants, which are more likely to be ethnically themed, inventive, edgy, and better-attuned to local preferences than their larger cloned counterparts. For chains and franchises whose foundation is sameness, homogeneity, and a one-size-fits-all model, a suddenly more adventurous restaurant patron does not spell good news at all.

Besides becoming increasingly willing to try something new, American consumers are feeling more locally connected. Almost 70 percent say they are more likely to visit a restaurant if it offers locally produced food items*. For independents, sourcing and incorporating locally-produced food is generally simple, manageable, and natural. For a multi-state restaurant chain, it runs absolutely contrary to their models of economy of scale and standardization that have, in the past, formed the basis of their profitability.

As well, consumers today are more health-conscious, and this is evident in their restaurant choices. A surprising 76 percent say they would be more likely to visit a restaurant if it offered healthful options*. Yes, fast food chains have been working to re-tool their menus to offer a few healthy options, but they lack the nimbleness of the local independent restaurant, and drag with them the baggage of being associated with unhealthy food offerings for decades.

Beyond expressing a heightened concern with healthy eating, the number of people who are choosing to follow diets, such as the vegan or gluten-free ones, which exclude large groups of foods, has been growing rapidly in recent years.

One source indicates that the percentage of people who identify as vegans has grown from approximately 1 percent of the population in 2009 to between 5 and 6 percent of the population in 2015. Similarly, the number of people who avoid eating gluten, either because they suffer from celiac disease or because they believe that gluten is generally unhealthy for them, has skyrocketed. Of course, people for whom the availability of vegetarian, vegan, or gluten-free options is a prerequisite to their decision to patronize a restaurant are not distributed evenly throughout the population; certain markets may have almost no members of this group and in others, they may constitute 30 percent or more of would-be diners. Local independent restaurants are able to take the measure of a given market and to tailor their concept to the sensibilities of their trade area (the geographic area surrounding it that accounts for the majority of its business). For a large multi-store chain, with restaurants in a variety of different markets, substantially modifying their menu to exactly fit the neighborhood surrounding each of their restaurants would be difficulty and contrary to their business model of standardization.

Among many restaurant consumers there is a palpable and growing anti-chain sentiment. This may be due to their desire for healthier food, an interest in local or regional cuisines, an expanded sense of adventurousness, or a manifestation of the increasingly buy-local culture. Whatever the reasons, there is a clear, and growing, segment of the population that prefers independent over chain or franchise restaurants.

In addition to rapidly shifting consumer preferences that favor local independents, the online landscape, in particular Yelp and similar crowd-sourced review sites that allow diners to post their thoughts about a dining experience, have had a huge impact on the restaurant business. Although they are viewed at best as a mixed blessing by many restaurant owners, I believe that, on the whole they serve to advantage smaller, local, lesser-known, and less-visible restaurants at the expense of larger chain restaurants. One of the main advantages that chain restaurants have enjoyed in the past is that for the consumer they represent a familiar, and therefore lower-risk, dining option. Whatever consumers thought about the quality and sameness of the food, they took comfort in knowing what to expect. For someone considering visiting a given restaurant for the first time, local independent restaurants, whose quality could vary dramatically from one to the next, represented a greater risk. Sometimes even finding them was difficult. If you were unfamiliar with the area, you might not stumble upon the local independent competitors, who traditionally have occupied less-pricey, less-visible real estate. And if you did happen to find them, there was a significant element of risk in making the selection. You knew absolutely nothing about the restaurant beyond what you might observe from the street and infer from the name.

Online crowd-sourced review sites allow hungry diners to quickly locate restaurants that are close by, and then read a sufficient number of reviews to decide whether or not to give the place a try. If the diner elects to try it, she has a pretty good idea what she is in for long before she gets to the door. This has worked to level the risk playing field and has been a boon to better, highly rated independents and, I believe, has worked to shift business their way, at the expense of larger, better-known chain restaurants.

After spending several days in San Diego recently researching local taco joints, and ready for a non-taco breakfast, we scanned online reviews and settled on a highly rated but distant breakfast spot. The

*neighborhood was out of the way and unappealing, and the build-
ing sad and uninviting. Once inside, though, we saw that the place
was hopping. We were seated quickly and immersed ourselves in
the intriguing menu. Within minutes a cheerful server took our order
and a few minutes later the food arrived. The flavors were fantastic
and the bill was inexpensive. Without online review sites and overwhelmingly positive reviews, we never would have found this place
and, if we had somehow driven by, we wouldn't have thought to
stop. I wondered, absent the glowing online reviews, how many of
their customers would be having breakfast somewhere else, somewhere more known, more visible, and better-located?*

Social media has the potential to draw attention to, promote, and
support small restaurants in ways unimaginable just a decade ago, ways
that can be nearly magical in their positive impact. In the past, forming a
community of ardently supportive patrons around a restaurant was a slow
and daunting task. Outside of the restaurant, the best the owner could
hope for was one-way communication, the owner disseminating information by mail, email, or paid advertising to customers or prospective customers, with little communication back from customer to owner, and with
virtually no peer-to-peer, customer-to-customer communication. It is this
banter, enthusiastic comments on new posts, and shared positive experiences that create buzz and grows customer enthusiasm and support for
the restaurant.

Facebook and other social media offer the independent restaurant
owner the unique and powerful ability to build a connected and self-
reinforcing community of fans. The restaurant's most ardent supporters, those who most identify with, and feel the strongest loyalty to, its
concept, execution, and location are given a place to belong, to share,
and to keep abreast of the establishment. As an avenue for advertising,
Facebook allows the business owner to target not just this community of
fans for promotions but also their friends and family, people likely to share

the same tastes and lifestyle, adding them to an ever-growing group of supporters. This is an independent restaurant owner's dream. Sure, large chains have the same access to social media. However, what they lack is a local, involved, and emotionally engaged fan base, a vocal community to rally around them. Without that, since the majority of customers in the restaurant business are local ones, the emotional immediacy, the buzz, and the bulk of the potential impact fails to materialize. Social media is a godsend to savvy independent restaurant owners and has the potential to benefit them over their multi-store chains in a big way.

The improving environment for independent restaurants is not limited to a rosy outlook for robust sales. At the same time that potential gross sales are growing, at least one major expense item is down. In many areas in the country the selling prices of commercially zoned buildings are 30 to 50 percent less than they were at the peak of the commercial real estate boom in 2007 and 2008. This has a major impact on restaurateurs; their third largest monthly expense, one surpassed only by the monthly costs of labor and food, is the cost of monthly rent or the mortgage payment. When you combine bargain-priced buildings with the current still very low long-term interest rates, you get the potential for a much-diminished mortgage payment and consequently a very low cost of occupancy. Additionally, selection is good. In many markets prime spaces are available for the first time in years.

For those for whom leasing makes more sense, rental rates in many markets have followed the market down and remain low and highly negotiable. The softer retail market means more landlords willing to consider shouldering the burden of remodeling, changing the use of, or making improvements to, vacant restaurant spaces and in some cases are willing to consider lease structures that tie the amount of rent to a restaurant's gross sales volume.

For many would-be first time restaurant owners, becoming self-employed has become less risky. An impediment to moving from employment to self-employment has been the issue of health insurance. Until recently leaving employment for self-employment meant leaving behind secure and affordable health insurance for hard-to-find, less-affordable, and lower-quality health insurance that was the self-employed person's only option. And if you happened to have a chronic health condition, it meant effectively no available health insurance. With the institution of the Affordable Care Act (ACA) in 2010, competitively priced insurance became available to the self-employed, even those with pre-existing conditions. For many of us, particularly those in middle age, ACA has eliminated one very big impediment to becoming a restaurant entrepreneur.

The restaurant industry is one where, to many people's surprise, smaller and single-store restaurants already dominate the market. In fact, nine out of 10 restaurants have fewer than 50 employees and seven out of 10 of all restaurants are single-store operations*.

For the local independent restaurant owner, we live in an amazing time. Industry sales are growing. There is a tsunami-like shift in consumer preferences afoot, which lopsidedly stands to benefit nimble independents. The rise in social media allows these neighborhood-aligned restaurants to build and interact with strong supportive fan bases. If ever there were a favorable environment in which to open an independent restaurant, it is today.

*National Restaurant Association, 2015 Restaurant Industry Pocket Fact Book

Two

Why later in your life may be the best time to start a restaurant

I have often joked that you can sit me down in a café or restaurant anywhere and I can point to the owner inside of a few minutes. My secret? I always look for the person with graying hair, moving quickly, and looking just a little bit nervous.

Later in life, even post-retirement, is a great time to start a restaurant; maybe the best time, and for many of us, the only time. This is the case for a host of reasons both situational and related specifically to aging.

FINALLY, SOME DISCRETIONARY TIME

Most of us find, as we approach middle age, that we have greater amounts of discretionary time. We may be able to fully retire, making available all of the hours previously devoted to work, or we may be able to diminish our work hours.

For many of us, if we had kids, by middle age they are largely grown and out of the house, giving us more time. And if there are adult kids still at home, well … they may find themselves suddenly employed in your new restaurant.

YOUR NETWORK OF CONNECTIONS IS AT ITS PEAK

By middle age most of us have developed a wide-ranging network of connections. We have a circle of close friends and much wider circles of casual affinity-based relationships, from a shared employer, congregation, hobby, or lifestyle. We have accrued a lifetime of business relationships, and have go-to people for real estate, insurance, and building trades. We have long ago separated the wheat from the chaff and we know who the reliable service providers are and who overcharges or lacks competence.

In establishing a restaurant, this vast network of friends and friends-of-friends will likely form the initial core group of our customers. As our friends share their experiences and enthusiasm with their friends, word spreads and a sustaining critical mass of customers becomes easier to develop.

The extended network of friends, acquaintances, and business relationships that we have accumulated by middle age may also serve as ideal ground for recruiting employees. Why hire strangers when there are already people in your network whom you know well and who know you?

IN MANY WAYS, YOUR INTELLIGENCE DOESN'T PEAK UNTIL MIDDLE AGE

Yes, our minds slow in many ways as we age, and certainly our memory becomes less sharp. However, in many other ways, ways essential to creating successful restaurants, we only begin to reach our peak mental skills in our fourth and fifth decade.

YOU ARE BETTER WITH MONEY

There is substantial evidence that our reasoning and problem-solving skills continue to improve into our fifties, particularly as relates to the skill with which we handle money. A study done for the Brookings Institute by Sumit Agarwal, an economist at the Federal Reserve Bank of Chicago, the middle-aged make smarter money decisions than their younger counter-parts. In particular, they are better at navigating complex financial trans-actions, managing credit card balances, and avoiding excess interest and fee payments. The best performance was by those study participants in their early 50s. Clearly, money smarts, an absolute necessity of creating and running independent restaurants, does not fully mature until about retirement age.

YOU UNDERSTAND AND CAN LEAD PEOPLE BETTER THAN EVER BEFORE

Your emotional and social intelligence, the smarts that allow you to imme-diately size up another person's emotional state, or to adroitly navigate complex interpersonal dilemmas – essential for hiring, motivating, retain-ing, and sometimes firing staff – grows as you age.

In a 2007 study published in the *Journal of Gerontology*, older and younger adults were presented with a series of hypothetical everyday problems (say, for example, an emotionally needy relative calls to talk just as you're leaving to meet up with friends, or you've won a free vacation, but the travel dates would mean missing a long-planned family party). The older adults were especially good at solving such interpersonal di-lemmas, often by choosing a path that skirted direct conflict. As we get older, our social intelligence keeps expanding, we get better at sizing up people, at understanding how relationships work.

While adults can most easily process new information at age 18, and while memory function peaks in your mid-20s, other key brain functions take much longer than previously thought to reach their pinnacles.

Research conducted by Joshua K. Hartshorne of Harvard University and Laura T. Germine of General Hospital of Boston, looked at various areas of cognition and understanding and found a wide range of ages when different emotional and social skill sets peak. For example, 12,000 people took a social intelligence test. The assignment was deceptively simple: just examine photographs of eyes and determine what emotion was being communicated. Surprisingly, social intelligence progressively improved during the 20s and 30s, with individuals in their 40s registering the highest test scores. This kind of social intelligence didn't start declining until subjects were well into their 60s. Dr. Hartshorne theorized that the long maturation cycle of this skill could be related to life experiences. Perhaps as our understanding of people deepens, this special cognitive resource just gets better?

Social intelligence is not even the last mental function to peak. Many cognitive abilities related to vocabulary, information, and comprehension reach their full potential even later – as late as age 70, according to some research.

IN MIDDLE AGE YOUR ABILITY TO QUICKLY MASTER NEW SKILLS IS AT ITS BEST

As your brain encounters new situations, it develops schemas—mental structures that allow you to identify and respond to similar circumstances when you come upon them again. By midlife you've accumulated an array of schemas that help you to quickly become oriented and to best adapt to novel situations by drawing on your storehouse of experience built up over time. Middle-aged restaurant owners, even with no prior restaurant experience, often quickly seem as though they have been in the business their entire lives.

IN MIDLIFE YOU LEARN TO MAINTAIN EMOTIONAL CALM AND BECOME MORE POSITIVE

Compared to their younger counterparts, middle-aged adults are able to maintain a more even keel emotionally. Psychologist Vasiliki Orgeta, PhD, in a 2009 study, evaluated younger and older adults and concluded that older adults (between ages 61 and 81) had more clarity about their feelings, made better use of strategies to regulate their emotions, and had a higher degree of control over their emotional impulses. In the often intense and high-pressure restaurant environment, being able to keep your cool is a distinct advantage.

YOU HAVE CLARITY AND A BETTER UNDERSTANDING OF THE BIG PICTURE

Your outlook grows rosier as you get older, as demonstrated by a study published recently in the journal *Psychology and Aging*. Laura Carstensen, a professor of psychology at Stanford University and director of the Stanford Center on Longevity, asked a group of subjects ages 18 to 94 to record their emotional states at five randomly chosen times each day for a one-week period. She repeated the procedure with the same partici-pants five years later, and then again five years after that. With the pas-sage of time, the study subjects reported more positive well-being and greater emotional stability. That may have been partly due to changes in how the brain – in particular, the emotion-processing center known as the amydgala – responds to positive and negative events. In a 2004 study, Carstensen scanned the brains of younger and older volunteers as they looked at cheerful, distressing, and neutral photographs. The amygdalae of younger subjects (ages 18 to 29) were activated equally by both the cheerful and distressing images, while the brains of the older subjects (between 70 and 90 years old) reacted much more strongly to the posi-tive pictures.

WE ARE BETTER ABLE TO SEE THE BIG PICTURE AND OUR PRIORITIES BECOME MORE CLEAR

As we age, we're better able to take the measure of a situation. An experi-ment published in the journal *Neuron* in 2005 provided a very literal dem-onstration of this ability: Psychologist Allison Sekuler, PhD, of McMaster University in Canada, presented younger and older subjects with com-puter screens showing moving images of varying shapes and shades. When the shapes were small and gray, younger people were able to point them out more quickly. But when they were large and high contrast, older individuals performed the task more quickly. Sekuler notes that young brains seem to be better at focusing on details to the exclusion of their surroundings, and more mature brains are able to take in the whole scene.

"Studies of the way adults perceive time suggest that we become increasingly aware that our years on this Earth are limited," notes Michael Marsiske, PhD, an associate professor of clinical and health psychology at the University of Florida and an expert on aging. "This awareness helps explain the choices that older adults tend to make: to spend time with a smaller, tighter circle of friends and family, to pay more attention to good news than to bad news, and to seek out positive encounters and avoid negative ones."

OVERALL MATURITY

Beyond the above specific intelligences and skill sets that appear to peak late in life, there is for most people a more generalized, but equally essential, blooming of an entire bundle of qualities that collectively we call wisdom.

The mature person keeps long-term commitments and has learned to delay gratification. If immoderate habits once existed, they have likely been long abandoned and replaced by ones that accrue, in the long term, to the person's benefit.

They have a depth that lets them remain relatively unmoved by either flattery or criticism; neither the most ecstatic customer praise nor the most wilting review on Yelp has much of an impact – their focus is on the big picture. As we age we become more and more secure in our sense of self.

By middle age we have cultivated a sense of humility. By that I don't mean thinking less of ourselves, but rather being open to input from others and grasping our own limitations. In middle age we place no value on drawing attention to ourselves and we understand how others make our success possible, which gives rise to gratitude for the people in our lives. In our maturity, and tendency toward arrogance, a costly, unhelpful, and off-putting trait in the restaurant business, has given way to humility.

In our maturity our decisions – how we treat our employees, customers, and suppliers – becomes based more on our values rather than our feelings of the moment. Our character eclipses our emotion.

Opening and managing restaurants in my fifties has been deeply satisfying and financially rewarding. I feel better suited for this work than perhaps any other I've undertaken in my professional life. Occasionally, wistfully, I am tempted to wish I had gone down this path earlier, maybe in my thirties or forties, instead of well into my fifties. But then I think about who I was in those years, preoccupied with child rearing, possessing much less maturity, clarity, and people skills, having less capital – both financial and social – and I realize I got into this business at exactly the right time, my middle age.

Resources: oprah.com/health/Aging-Brain-Facts-Do-You-Get-Smarter-as-You-Age#ixzz43jTyVPeS

Three

Is owning a restaurant right for you?

Are you well-suited to owning a restaurant? Will you be good at it? Will the process of conceiving, researching, planning, designing, opening, and running a restaurant be fun, challenging, and rewarding for you? Being a restaurateur is a demanding occupation, one requiring a great diversity of skills, resources, and assets, and it is not for everyone.

Here are the qualities that I see as indispensable to successful restaurateurs:

Vision: It is essential that you are able to develop a vision of how to create something singular and special. Locally independent restaurants that compete successfully with vastly better-funded, better-researched, and more-established national chains have at least one thing in common: Their owners have managed to create something beyond the ordinary, something singular, something that resonates with their customers. Be it a unique environment, a one-of-a-kind product, a tangible expression of an aspect of the owner's personality, to thrive you must create something memorable. Having a strong vision and a commitment to it is essential to your restaurant's survival. Independent restaurants that offer nothing particularly special are doomed. After all, a franchise or chain store can offer "nothing special" and do it cheaper, more uniformly, and more efficiently than you will ever be able to. An ice cream shop that makes ice cream that is no better quality than the least expensive supermarket brand, a coffee shop with a blah interior and sub-par espresso drinks, a café serving the same old food the same way – none of them will prosper because there is nothing special there. The owner's concept lacked a vison that would make the establishment stand out and excel.

If you don't have the desire to create something unique, excellent, wonderful, and maybe quirky, something that is a very personal extension of who you are, something that expresses your deepest values, then I would suggest politely that opening a restaurant is not your highest calling.

Practicality: While having an overarching artistic vision and an eye for detail in the execution of that vision is essential, creating and running a profitable restaurant also requires abundant common sense and a disciplined practicality. Have a strong vision? Good. Blow the operating reserves you may need to make it through your first year of operation so you can get exactly the brand new kitchen equipment or high-end finishes for your dining room that you crave. Disastrous.

Some financial capital: In a later chapter we will look at a variety of different restaurant approaches and the vastly differing amounts of capital each will require. For now suffice it to say that to start up any restaurant venture, in order to purchase equipment and food supplies, and to operate until you reach profitability, you will need some financial capital. If you have none, you are probably better off waiting to open your restaurant until you save up some, rather than starting with very little capital reserves, or by borrowing all of your startup capital and soon finding yourself suffocating under an onerous monthly debt service to pay it back.

Lots of friends: Opening a restaurant is a time when you will want to draw on, and involve, people from every sphere of social connection that you have. Your extended social networks, be they congregation or a group of people you know because you share the same recreational pursuit with, can be of great benefit to you. Those many hundreds of loose friends, distant relatives, and acquaintances you might have on Facebook or similar social media can be recruited for soft openings and will comprise much of your initial customer base. By encouraging them to post images of themselves at your new restaurant you can gain popularity within a subset of people who have in common their connection with you.

For the last decade, my primary recreation has been dancing Argentine tango. I am closely connected with several hundred local dancers and, enabled by Facebook, have a loose connection with about 1,000 people with the same passion. This preexisting community has been hugely helpful in establishing my restaurants over the years. Tango dancers, when visiting Albuquerque, will inevitably post photos of themselves eating at one of my restaurants, which enhances our exposure. And in the early days, almost all of my staff was recruited from the tango community, giving us an all-dancer staff.

Having a very large preexisting network of friends, acquaintances, and associates may not be absolutely essential, but it makes getting a restaurant established much easier.

Availability and flexibility of time: Initially any restaurant startup, particularly your first, will require a monumental investment of time. However, over time increased cash flow allows for hiring more employees, and if you are able to effectively delegate, the time required of you will decrease. But your schedule will still need to be flexible and open. The buck stops with you, and that may mean having to step in at any time, with no notice, to substitute for a suddenly sick employee or to address a critical operational problem. You are best suited for this if you have no other fixed, inflexible, time commitments such as a day job.

Basic business skills: The business math and related financial concepts you will need are not particularly difficult, consisting mostly of simple ledger accounting, and calculation of expense ratios. However, it is a requirement not an option. Yes, you will likely outsource payroll and some book keeping and tax-related tasks but still, independent restaurants operate on relatively small net profit margins and without constant income and expense ratio monitoring, and fine tuning, you can quickly find yourself in a money-losing freefall. If you are not comfortable with some level of math-based conceptualization and accounting being a part of your weekly and daily life, restaurant ownership will likely not be a good fit for you.

Comfort with leadership and management: The vast majority of restaurants will have employees. Having employees puts you in a position of hiring, inspiring, managing, setting the culture for, and occasionally disciplining and firing people. If you are not comfortable with this, if you don't enjoy the leadership opportunity, if you are total uncomfortable with the prospect of disciplining and firing employees, any sort of employee-concentrated business may not feel be a good fit for your personality. Similarly, if you are impatient and hot-tempered by nature, and would have trouble maintaining composure and equanimity in a crisis, and would have trouble following a predetermined protocol for discipline and firing employees, owning a restaurant absolutely will not be a good fit for you.

Humility: I wrote this book for people contemplating opening their first restaurants, which usually means someone with little or no prior restaurant ownership experience, which in turn means people who have everything to learn. Your ability to seek out, solicit, and then assimilate input from dozens of people, each of whom may have one or two areas of profound yet narrow expertise – your refrigeration technician, line cooks, pest control technician, coffee roaster, espresso machine technician, health department inspector, suppliers, etc. – is critical to your ability to administer the whole. Also, the casual observations of one of your customers with no restaurant experience, when heard without defensiveness, can be invaluable. An absence of humility, a lack of openness, do not bode well for restaurant ownership success.

Curiosity: Restaurants are amazingly multi-faceted. They are rooted in the timeless act of food preparation, which in itself is an amalgam of chemistry, craft, and artistry. The business of restaurants encompasses commodity pricing, real estate, utility rates, and is entirely predicated on effective marketing. It is easy to acquire some fundamental knowledge of this or that area, and then to ossify, to hit a knowledge or skill ceiling, and stop growing. The rate of change and evolution in the restaurant business is a high one; state-of-the-art marketing changes by the month, food preferences evolve, equipment changes. How do you stay current and on top of your game? Curiosity. An abiding curiosity about everything that forms the restaurant world, the mechanical (e.g., how do refrigerators work and can I fix them myself?), everything culinary (e.g., how does baking powder work?), everything marketing (e.g., who is my most profitable demographic for this store and how can I reach it?), everything financial (e.g., could I tweak my menu in a way that would reduce my labor to gross sales ratio?), and everything psychological (e.g., how can I get more "buy in" from my employees?) is needed.

Affability: Perhaps it goes without saying, but being grumpy will not serve you well in owning your restaurant. In the real world, *Seinfeld's* "soup Nazi" wouldn't be able to stay in business for a week. Customers want a comfortable, warm experience. Interacting with a grumpy owner, noticing tension in the air, or overhearing unkind words hurled at an employee, will poison that atmosphere. As well, employees are disinclined to work in a tense, chilly, environment. Affability is important in attracting and keeping both your best employees and your best customers.

Determination: It is rare that a restaurant is a success right out of the gate. There will always be setbacks, large and small, and sometimes a long period before profitability is reached. There will likely be major equipment failures, sudden changes in staff, inexplicable slow days, and disappointments of every type. In the first years of my first restaurant I experienced a fire, a flood, and a floor refinishing project that unexpectedly expanded in scope about tenfold, shutting the restaurant down for a week.

A deep resilience, a determination to keep "getting back on the horse" will be required. If you get discouraged easily, if you don't naturally take the long view, owning a restaurant will not be a good fit.

Each of us is unique and we all have mixes of strengths and weaknesses, and we all have the ability to change and grow. Still, it is worth pausing and reflecting on your particular attributes and how they square with what you will likely encounter as the owner of a newly minted restaurant.

Four

How much money will it take?

This chapter should allow you very early on to decide upon a general direction to take as it relates to real estate that is feasible with your budget.

To open your restaurant, will you need millions, hundreds of thousands, tens of thousands, or as little as a few thousand dollars?

My intent in this chapter is to give you a rough template to compare your actual startup cost under a range of different real estate scenarios. This will help you to, from early on, align the approach you will take regarding the real estate in opening your restaurant with the amount of your available capital.

Matching your available capital, no matter how small or large the amount might be, with a realistic estimate of expenses in opening your new venture is critical. A frequently-cited reason for restaurant failure is the exhaustion of capital in the pre-opening phase, leaving little or none available to sustain the restaurant until it becomes established and profitable.

The largest variable in startup costs is real estate. Fortunately, in the restaurant business there are approaches that match almost every budget. Let's take a look at a number of scenarios, beginning with the most expensive and ending with the least expensive.

BUYING A BUILDING

In any market there are existing restaurant facilities for sale, often with functional commercial kitchens and furnishings included as part of the deal. The advantages of purchasing an existing facility are many. Likely the building is zoned correctly for restaurant use, and the building has been inspected many times by the relevant food safety and building safety officials as an operating restaurant. It may have conditions, such as signage or bathroom configuration, which would not be allowed if you were building a restaurant today but may well be "grandfathered in." Also, there may be a history of the performance of the restaurant formerly housed in the building, which may provide insight into the demand from the surrounding market area.

Conceptually, the cost to purchase an existing restaurant facility and use it as the location for your new restaurant can be calculated by doing the following:

1. Determine your "cash out of pocket" required for your real estate purchase. To do this, take the purchase price of the property, subtract any amount you are able to finance, and then add to that any costs of acquisition (inspections, transfer taxes, attorney fees, etc.).

   Example: If you purchase your building for $500,000 and have $10,000 in acquisition costs, and are able to borrow 70 percent of the purchase price of the building ($350,000) then your required cash out of pocket would be calculated as follows: $500,000 (the building purchase price) - $350,000 (the amount you are able to borrow for the building purchase) = $150,000 (your down payment for the building) + $10,000 (your acquisition costs) = $160,000 (your total cash out of pocket).

2. Add to that any soft costs (architectural fees, engineering fees, cost of permitting, etc.) associated with any remodeling required to remodel the building to make it suitable for your particular concept.
3. Add to that any hard costs (the actual cost of construction) for the above remodeling.
4. Add to that the costs to hold the building (monthly mortgage payment, property taxes, insurance, maintenance, etc.) from the time you purchase it until you complete any required remodel, open for business, and the business becomes established and can pay the reoccurring costs associated with owning the building. If you pay cash for the building, the holding costs may be minimal (typically property taxes, insurance, and maintenance), but if you are financing the building you will need to figure in the monthly cost of the monthly debt service.
5. Add to that the cost of any equipment that you will need to replace or add to the existing equipment in order to implement your concept. This includes your kitchen and refrigeration equipment, furnishings, sales counters, displays, POS system, sound system, etc.
6. Add to that any costs associated with the installation of various systems including your POS system, security system, internet, audio system, etc.
7. Add to that your cost of your initial food and supplies.
8. Add to that the initial payroll until the venture becomes established and can meet its own payroll.
9. Add to that the cost of any initial advertising and promotion.
10. Add to that a large set-aside or contingency fund for anything unexpected such as delays in opening, delays in reaching projected sales, and/or profitability goals.

Your total costs to purchase an existing restaurant facility obviously will vary greatly with the real estate market in your area and the extent to which you have to modify the building for your use. The biggest take away from the above is the need to make sure you have enough capital in reserve to see the project through to long past opening prior to making a commitment to purchase the building.

Purchasing an existing food service facility does reduce many risks and expenses associated with converting a building from a prior non-restaurant use. Because it eliminates or substantially reduces some variables, such as the costs associated with a major remodel needed to legally change the use of the building, purchasing such a facility makes calculating an accurate estimate of total capital needed much easier. However, it may also be one of your most expensive options because the value that the real estate market places on the building as a restaurant may be significantly higher than the amount for which you could purchase a similar non-restaurant building and convert it to restaurant use. If you are in the financial position to purchase a building for your restaurant, you may want to consider buildings that have not previously housed restaurants. Doing so will open up the number of buildings available to you on the market, may allow you to create equity by converting the building to a restaurant use, and may allow for a more interesting overall facility, one uniquely tailored to your concept.

In purchasing a building not previously used as a restaurant and converting it to restaurant use, the costs are the same as the above expense tally, except that the scale of, and budget for, the remodel will likely be much larger, as will be the time required to compete it. You will also need to purchase all kitchen equipment rather than only that which you would otherwise be replacing or adding. In purchasing a building and converting it for restaurant use you should also set aside a much larger contingency budget due to the greater potential for delays with the expanded scope of the design, construction drawing, permitting, construction, inspection, and approval process.

LEASING SPACE FOR YOUR RESTAURANT

Purchasing a building may not be possible and, even when it is, may not always be the best option. Being willing to lease, rather than being willing to consider only buildings available for purchase, opens up many more possible locations and may reduce your financial risk and, of course, can dramatically reduce the total capital required for the venture. As with purchasing a building, when leasing you can either lease a building that previously has been used as a restaurant or one that never has been used as a restaurant.

If you are able to find a vacant space or building that housed a restaurant or other food service facility previously, your capital requirements will need to cover:

1. The security deposit and any prepaid rent required per the lease agreement.
2. Any modifications to, or remodeling of, the space to make it work for your concept.
3. The rent from the time you take occupancy until the restaurant reaches profitability (minus any months of free rent landlord may be willing to offer in exchange for a long-term lease).
4. Any equipment that you will need to add to the existing equipment.
5. Reserves for payroll from pre-opening and training to until the establishment becomes established and profitable.
6. The cost of initial promotions and advertising.

If you lease a building that has not housed a restaurant previously, you can add to the above:

1. Whatever portion of the soft and hard costs associated with the remodel that will not be paid for by the landlord, per your negotiated lease.

2. Whatever portion of the rent you are responsible for per your negotiated lease during the design, remodel, permitting, and inspection period.
3. The cost of all equipment and all furnishings.

"POP-UP" RESTAURANTS

The absolute least expensive option for opening a restaurant is a pop-up. This is a model of restaurant that exists under the roof of another restaurant, using their equipment and facility, during the hours that they are not open.

One of the economic trends that has surfaced, and become economically significant, in the last 10 years or so, is that of the shared economy, where owners put into play and monetize underutilized assets. This is the bases of Airbnb, where property owners offer short-terms rentals of unused rooms in their home, and of ride-share services such as Uber and Lyft where people put their personal automobiles to use offering transportation to strangers. Pop-up restaurants are the restaurant industry's manifestation of this trend.

A restaurant offering only breakfast and lunch may be a perfect opportunity for a dinner or very late-night pop-up restaurant. Conversely, a dinner restaurant may present an opportunity for a breakfast or even a weekend-only brunch pop-up venture. For an existing restaurant, leasing space for a pop-up operating during their closed hours can be a great way of generating additional income or splitting the rent with another non-competing business.

Compared to other location options, opening a pop-up can be amazingly inexpensive. The capital requirements are:

1. The cost of any additional equipment not provided by the master restaurant.

2. The initial cost of the food you will be offering.
3. Reserves for labor until the operation becomes established.
4. The initial costs of advertising and promotion.

Five

Capitalization: How are you going to fund your restaurant?

It is essential for you to have a comfortable alignment between your restaurant concept and the total amount of funding you are able to bring to the table. Running out of money midway through the process of opening your restaurant would be a nightmare. In this chapter we will explore several options for raising the capital necessary to establish your restaurant and discuss some of the potential implications and consequences of each path.

FINANCE IT YOURSELF FROM SAVINGS

The most straightforward option is to fund the entire venture yourself, from savings, even if the amount you have available is small. This approach has a number of significant advantages and even may increase the odds of your restaurant succeeding significantly.

Self-financing gives you wiggle room, space, and time to maneuver without the crippling pressure of a monthly loan repayment. Independent restaurants have average net profit margins in the range of 10 to 12 percent of gross sales. Particularly in the early months and years, before your maximum gross sales volume is reached, and before you have had the opportunity to fine-tune your operations and pricing to enhance your profitability, your net profit may be much less, or zero, or you may bleed money. Imposing the burden of debt service on your bottom line, the monthly payment on a loan for equipment or other startup expenses, may mean the difference between staying afloat and sinking.

Viewed another way, if you have no debt, the portion of your bottom line that would otherwise be allocated to monthly debt service can function as a buffer, providing a margin of safety between you and a potential negative cash flow. This cash-flow cushion can buy you time to adjust your concept, marketing, equipment, and staffing without the pressure of negative cash flow. Given the choice between a very modest venture that can be financed entirely from your savings and a larger-scale, more ambitious or prestigious one that requires incurring debt, I would strongly advise the former.

The potential negatives of borrowing funds for a first-time restaurant startup are many and, I think, generally underappreciated. All of us, no matter how many restaurants we have opened, will make substantial errors at the beginning. By avoiding borrowing funds, and forcing ourselves to work at a small scale, with perhaps initially a very humble endeavor, the costs of our mistakes are likewise small-scale and bearable. There is always time for expansion once the bugs are worked out and the formula is fine-tuned. It may be best to keep the option of obtaining outside financing untapped until and unless your first venture is a runaway success.

Failure is always an option. People don't like to hear this. It has become a fashionable belief that boundless positive thinking will somehow reduce the likelihood that a given venture may ultimately fail. It won't. Worse yet, being overly optimistic may blind you to economic realities that you might have otherwise taken note of. Customer preferences, costs, neighborhood demographic, and the economy all change with time. Failure is, and will always be, a possibility to be incorporated into any wise and realistic business person's planning. That being the case, having your smallish new restaurant fail, and taking a relatively small loss on cash that you invested, is far preferable to having a massive-scale restaurant fail and leaving you with debt that might foreclose the pos-sibility of future ventures.

EQUITY FINANCING OR DEBT FINANCING?

If you choose to finance your new restaurant, you have two distinctly dif-ferent ways to go about this: equity financing and debt financing.

EQUITY FINANCING

In equity financing, in exchange for some amount of money, the investor owns some portion of a business and its assets. There is no loan. You might think of equity financing as being similar to purchasing stock in an enterprise; you actually purchase a percentage ownership that deter-mines your right to some percentage of future profits and potentially to future profit in the event of a sale of the business. Just as a corporation may have multiple stockholders, you may have multiple equity partners.

Taking on equity partners in your venture can result in much greater initial startup capital than you would have using only self-financing. Some concepts have unavoidably large frontend expenses for equipment, con-struction, and taking on a few large, or many small, equity partners can produce the requisite capital. And, bringing in partners can also result in an accumulation of experience, expertise, and available time and energy beyond what you might otherwise have at your disposal.

Taking on equity partners brings with it a number of potential prob-lems. To some degree, having different partners will mean having dif-ferent, often competing, visions as to the restaurant's concept and the execution of the concept. As well, different partners may have vastly dif-ferent levels of motivation, expertise, drive, and commitment. This can create strain on the partnership either immediately or over time.

Even the most compatible partners may not share the same life tra-jectory for long. Given several partners, one may for instance, decide to relocate, get divorced, suffer ill health, or wish to pursue other unrelated business options. No matter how good the initial compatibility and intent over time people's lives, finances, and interests will each change independently. Therefore, it is important, before the formation of any partnership, to discuss and decide how the partnership can be dissolved, if the partners so elect, and how one partner might go about liquidating their interest in the partnership either to the remaining partners or to a new investor. In forming a financial partnership with equity investors, counsel from an attorney with substantial experience in partnership formation and dissolution is vital.

If you decide to seek investors by offering some sort of security to them, for example, stock in your venture, you must take great care not to run afoul of the relevant federal Securities and Exchange Commission (SEC) and individual state regulations. Likely, if the security instrument is not registered with the SEC, you will not be able to advertise it to the public at large or to solicit investors with whom you do not already have a relationship. If you are considering advertising to seek investors, familiarize yourself with the applicable SEC and state securities regulations and consult knowledgeable counsel first.

DEBT FINANCING
In debt financing you keep complete ownership of the venture and money is borrowed and secured by either the restaurant assets or some other asset, such as your residence or other real property. For most people, starting their own independent restaurant for the first time, a loan secured by that restaurant and its future earnings, would be too risky a proposition for most lenders. This is particularly the case in the very risk-averse lending environment of the last decade.

A more likely option is borrowing against some other asset, say, stock or real estate, unrelated to the restaurant venture, which reduces the risk to the lender by providing it with better and more liquid security, and which should translate into a better interest rate for you. As well, the amortization period, with a loan secured by real estate, might be much longer than with a purely business loan, giving you the option for a lower monthly loan payment. Additionally, if you are borrowing against your primary residence, the interest may be tax deductible.

CROWDFUNDING

In the crowdfunding model, as popularized by Kickstarter, Indiegogo, and similar websites, you propose and promote your idea online, in the form of a campaign, and in return receive pledges from participants. Those making the pledges, and eventually contributing the money if the campaign reaches its goals, receive incentives such as gifts and premiums good at your eventual restaurant.

There have been a number of spectacular successes with some restaurants raising several hundreds of thousands of dollars. Many more raise no money at all. Crowdfunding is not free money. It only results in actual funding when your campaign reaches its pledge goal.

Crowdfunding campaigns are typically 30 days in duration and are extremely labor intensive, both in terms of preparing for and in administering them throughout the campaign period. A time budget of 150 hours is a minimum. Typically the campaign is executed by a team, with a project manager coordinating it. One member of the team might handle the photography and videography, another the social media side of the campaign and press releases.

How much money should you ask for? This is a critical question in a crowdfunding campaign, because to receive any funding you must hit your pledge goal. Some of the most successful campaigns are tied to the acquisition of a tangible goal that would result from the success of the campaign, say acquiring a walk-in cooler, or making some other improvement with a modest price tag.

Another approach to selecting a reasonable goal amount is to review previous crowdfunding campaigns in your area to get a realistic sense of the size of goals for campaigns that have met their goals. If you find that no restaurant campaigns in your area have raised more than $50,000, it makes no sense to set your goal much higher than that, unless your circumstances are very different; say, if you were trying to raise money for an expansion to a very popular existing restaurant that already has a large fan base and presence on social media.

You must figure into the equation the cost of the reward or premium you are offering relative to the amount raised. If the cost to your of providing the rewards or premium is high relative to the goal of the campaign, it may not be worth doing.

Your rewards or incentives should be offered at an array of different tiers, to appeal to people of different means and levels of interest in being involved. For example, you might have different rewards for $20, $50, $100, and $500 contributions. Like so much else, the market and supply and demand will impact the size of the incentive you offer so be sure to research similar and competing campaigns conducted in your area.

In crowdfunding momentum is huge. Hitting goals in the first few days of your campaign dramatically increase your odds of success. A launch party is a great way to begin your campaign with a bang and convert your attendees into eager advocates for your campaign. Use your launch party to introduce your products and to personally meet supporters. Invite potential customers, business contacts, associates, and people from your social network. Post photos of your launch party on social media and encourage your attendees to do the same.

Throughout your campaign the goal is to tell, and show, your story. Use appealing imagery, professional photographs of your new restaurant space, and food to entice. Use social media to extend your reach.

Much like political campaigns, successful crowdfunding campaigns will need to be constantly tweaked and altered in order to achieve maximum efficacy.

Consider professional help with your crowdfunding. There are agencies with a very enviable success rate in orchestrating campaigns as well as online classes on crowdfunding specific to restaurant owners.

Resources: The Plinth Agency *offers 30-min crowdfunding classes designed specifically for food entrepreneurs called PlinthAcademy.com.*

Six

Developing your restaurant concept

Your concept for your restaurant is your overarching vision for it, which includes: the core cuisine idea, the type of service used for taking orders and for delivering food, the ways the food will be prepared, the menu item price range, the feel and style of the place, how it will operate, the hours it will be open, and the type of customer you hope to attract and retain.

Edgar Allan Poe once said, "A short story must have a single mood and every sentence must build towards it." Similarly, in developing a winning restaurant concept, every sensory experience – the exterior appearance of the restaurant, the feel of the space when you enter, the colors, the smells, the lines, the style, the interaction with the staff, the menu, the food, the presentation – should all work in harmony to build toward one unique, pleasing experience for the diner. Every aspect of your concept should contribute to a compelling consistent harmonious whole, like a well-composed piece of music or a well-written short story.

A great restaurant concept is one that is well-researched, well-developed, and a good fit for the tastes, preferences, and means of the potential customers in your surrounding trade area. Once complete, your concept will serve as a guide in your navigation of key decisions, particularly your location selection. A well-articulated concept will guide you in your staffing, marketing, decorating, sourcing, and a plethora of other smaller decisions. A restaurant concept that is unclear or not clearly articulated risks a resulting restaurant that feels muddled, incongruous, and lacking focus.

What drives a restaurant concept? If you begin with a concept and proceed to find a trade area in which to locate it, the likely drivers of your concept might be either trendiness – certain concepts are currently on the ascendancy while others are on the decline – or your personal knowledge of and affinity for a certain style of food. If you are beginning with a location and developing a concept in response, the drivers of your concept will primarily relate to the demographic (age, income, etc.) and psychographic characteristics of the residents of your surrounding trade area.

THOSE THINGS THAT EXPRESS YOUR CONCEPT

What are the instruments in your orchestra that you can employ to create a masterful composition? What are the colors in your paint box with which to render art? Below are the primary elements you have to work with to express and orchestrate your restaurant concept.

The food: The core of your restaurant, the primary reason customers come and return, is the food you serve. A successful food concept must be cohesive. There is nothing that appears as random and all elements contribute to a compelling whole. And, without sacrificing its sense of whole, an ideal food concept should be inclusive, providing options for subsets of customers with specialized diets (vegan, gluten-free) and tame, risk-averse, food sensibilities.

Your food concept must resonate with current food preferences and yet, to be sustainable, must not be reliant on novelty to too identified with a "here today, gone tomorrow" trend.

Customers select restaurants based on emotion more than based on analytical thinking, so your food concept must emotionally connect and resonate with your prospective customers.

In my first restaurant, Tia Betty's, I worked to reproduce a very localized retro style of cuisine that many people in our area are familiar with from the home cooking they know from their youth. The most common comments we receive about the food are, "This tastes like my grandmother's cooking" and "This smells like my grandmother's house." After I had heard this comment from many people, all of whom were born and raised in our state, I knew my food concept for that restaurant had a strong emotional resonance within, at least, a narrow demographic.

The details of your food concept have further implications. How each item is prepared determines your kitchen design and equipment choices. The ingredients you use, their price and availability, will largely determine the price point of your food items, which in turn adds to or limits the appeal of your concept to different customer groups.

The atmosphere: The atmosphere in your restaurant, how it feels to be there, is an essential aspect of your concept. The elements of atmosphere include:

Architecture: What does the exterior of the restaurant communicate? Does it communicate something about your core concept and give the customer a hint or promise of what to expect inside? Once inside, what is the first impression? Is the organizational logic (Where do I sit? How do I order?) immediately apparent? What does the quality and thoughtfulness of the interior design communicate about the service and food that the customer is about to receive? Are all visual elements working in harmony to further your overall restaurant concept?

Color: Color design plays an important role in both the interior and exterior of your building. Psychologically warm colors stimulate appetite while cool ones suppress it, though an appealing and sophisticated color design will have both warm and cool elements. For most people, unless they have a trained or naturally very refined eye for color, it is well worth soliciting help with color selection. You might hire a color consultant, usually someone with a background in interior design. Another alternative is to select a pre-designed palette of colors and adapt them to the elements of your building. Several paint companies offer free publications with photos of commercial and residential properties painted using palette of colors that their designers have assembled. The advantage of this approach is that the harmony of the colors is pretty much guaranteed, from the photos you can get a good sense of the final outcome, and you will get the exact color shown in the palette and building photos. How you adapt the scheme to your building is up to you.

Hiring a color consultant for two of my restaurants is one of the most cost-effective things I have ever done. In my second restaurant, La Waffleria, after a great deal of thought my color consultant suggested essentially no color, that I leave the dining room white and add a glossy black baseboard and chair railing. The result was simple, visually clean, yet elegant and harmonious with the 1920s vintage of the property. Best yet, executing the interior design cost under $500!

Lighting: If you have too little light at tables patrons will struggle to read the menu. Too much light and your restaurant feels institutional, sterile, and uncomfortable. Unusual, visually striking, lighting design offers some of the most impact of any element in creating a compelling restaurant interior.

Visual access to kitchen: There is nothing quite like being able to look into a restaurant's kitchen and watch your food being prepared. The open burners, or the glow emanating from a wood-fired pizza oven, harken back to ancient times and offer a sense of hearth and home. There is also something both reassuring and entertaining about watching a busy kitchen as you await your food. Personally I find kitchens with no visual access disconcerting. Consider whether some visual access to the kitchen from your dining room might further your concept.

Sound: The acoustical environments of restaurants can run the gamut from comforting and entertaining to abrasive and annoying. Sound forms a significant part of the dining experience and it can work for or against you.

Music can be not only relaxing for your patrons but can underline and reinforce your key concept. In the early years of my restaurant Tia Betty's we played strictly 1940s big band music, which seemed harmonious with our retro, 1940's theme. The Hard Rock Café chain plays well-known top 40 bands, creating both an edgy and familiar audio trademark.

Think about music that will further your concept but above all avoid music that might be perceived as intrusive, offensive, or that is played at a volume that some patrons might find intrusive or abrasive.

In my third restaurant, El Cotorro, we rotate the background music between a number of different greats of the Latin jazz, in general, and Cuban jazz, in particular. It's hard for me to imagine myself in that restaurant without hearing Tito Puente, Compay Segundo, or Ibrahim Ferrer and I hope my customers feel the same. The sound is an inseparable part of the experience.

If you have any sort of open or exhibition kitchen it is inevitable that kitchen sounds, the clattering of pots and pans, the chatter of the cooks, the chopping and prepping of ingredients, will fill the dining room. For the most part this is a good thing, creating a sense of energy and anticipation for the diners. However, not all sounds are welcome. If an open kitchen is part of the concept care must be taken to limit any conversation – vulgarities and unsavory stories – that might take place in the kitchen and be overheard in the dining room.

Busy dining rooms can be major noise generators. While some amount of ambient noise and chatter can provide a stimulating sense of a busy dining room, too much background noise is distinctly unpleasant. If you have low ceilings, mostly hard unbroken walls and ceilings, consider mitigating the sound level with the installation of low-cost acoustic panels, fabrics, curtains, or the like.

Smell: In furthering your concept, smell can play a decidedly negative or positive role. In the negative category would be various non-food smells: cleaning compounds, disinfecting sprays, and anything diners might find overpowering or "chemical," Smells that positively advance your goals include baking smells (bread, cookies, pizza, etc.) and the cooking smells of some food items.

PAIRING YOUR CONCEPT WITH YOUR TRADE AREA.

When you have a basic idea of your concept, developed without a specific location in mind, you will need to figure out what types of customers will be drawn to a restaurant expressing the concept you have come up with. You will want to have a good understanding of the demographic's characteristics and psychographic segments (see appendix for psychographic segmentation category descriptions) that your concept will appeal to, which will guide your site selection process.

If you are developing your restaurant concept with a specific location in mind, you will want to incorporate everything you can learn about the people in the surrounding area, the relevant demographics and psychographics, in your development of your restaurant concept.

In either case incorporating everything you can learn about the behaviors of your potential customers either in your site selection or concept development when you already have a site in mind, will be essential to achieving a good fit between your concept and your potential customers. We discuss how to acquire and use both demographic and psychographic segmentation information in the chapter on site selection.

WHAT OPERATIONAL STRATEGY WILL YOU USE?

Once you have your basic restaurant concept defined, it's important to nail down an operational or service strategy. Your restaurant will probably fall into one of the below basic service categories:

- **Fine dining** offers a highly designed upscale interior, highly trained chefs, a full range of alcoholic beverages, exceptional customer service, and a high price point.
- **Casual dining** offers full table service but with a more affordable menu in comparison to fine dining, which results in a broader customer base. Casual dining restaurants are typically seen as family-friendly, further extending the customer base.
- **Fast-casual or limited-service restaurants** are typically perceived to offer better food quality and improved service over quick-service places. Fast-casual-concept restaurants' menus tend to be less extensive but also less expensive than casual dining restaurants and counter service is the norm.
- **Quick-service restaurants** are focused on convenience and speed of service. These restaurants typically have simple décor, inexpensive food items, and fast counter service.

Most food concepts can be delivered using any of the above concepts. For instance, a Mexican food concept could be executed in one way as a quick-service restaurant with an emphasis on speed and low cost, or in a fast casual context with greater freshness, better presentation, and perhaps bolder flavors with a more appealing atmosphere, or in a casual dining context with table service and a slightly higher price point, or in a fine dining context, where the cuisine might be more refined, specific to only one or two regions in Mexico, and prepared by trained chefs rather than by line cooks.

The likely determinants in selecting an operational strategy will be the income demographics of the residents and daytime workers in your trade area. As well, existing competition may figure into the decision. For example, if an area has a large number of daytime workers who are being served by quick service restaurants, maybe there is an opening for a new restaurant with a fast-casual concept, for the segment of potential customers who are more quality or flavor conscious.

QUIRKINESS – AN INDEPENDENT'S SECRET WEAPON

A word I often hear used to describe my own restaurants is "quirky," perhaps a response to some of their unconventional and idiosyncratic facets. The descriptors seem to always appear in a positive context.

Customers – the ones that seek out independent restaurants, anyway – seem to have an openness and appreciation for the charmingly offbeat and unexpected, as long as it does not detract from the core of their experience, good food, service, and atmosphere.

A competitive advantage that independent, single-store restaurants enjoy is being able to indulge themselves in a bit of whimsy, playfulness, or oddness in a way that would be unacceptably risky for a multi-store chain wishing to fit into diverse trade areas in numerous different markets. Use this to your benefit! Whether it be unusual art on the wall, odd staff costumes, or attention-getters such as a zip line that the order taker uses to sail the orders back into the kitchen, express your playfulness. Your customers will likely appreciate it, and it will set you apart from more tame cloned restaurants.

AN EXERCISE IN UNDERSTANDING RESTAURANT CONCEPTS

Visit two of your favorite restaurants and two restaurants that you feel are subpar. Sit in each restaurant and carefully review the menu, décor, and operational style of the restaurant. Then write a one-page description of what you believe to be the underlying concept of each restaurant. For the better restaurants, does the task flow easily? For the subpar restaurants, is it more difficult to discern an underlying, cohesive concept?

For each restaurant, which elements seem to advance the concept and which seem to detract from it?

In the evolution of your vision for your restaurant, there is likely nothing more imperative then getting the concept right. Don't rush it or marry a concept too soon. I have spent weeks researching, developing, fleshing out, and even creating menus based on restaurant concepts that I have ultimately abandoned, after eventually seeing their limitation or after identifying a different concept that seemed better suited for the site I had was working with.

Resources

1. *NR Media Social Restaurant Podcast – Well-Defined Restaurant Concepts*
2. *https://www.spreaker.com/user/nateriggs/035-well-defined-restaurant-concepts*

Seven

Creating and pricing your menu

Your restaurant's menu is its offer to your customer. It says, "Here is what we are, here is what we have to offer, and here is what we ask in return."

In a sense, nearly everything about your restaurant, your concept, your values, your manner of cooking, your aesthetic, and your ability to organize are all communicated by your menu. From a marketing standpoint, a menu is one of your most powerful tools. It is at the right place at the right time, in front of your ideal prospect, a hungry diner already in your establishment.

CONSIDERATIONS IN DEVELOPING YOUR MENU
Your menu is directly linked to, and has implications for, every aspect of your operation. It must then be developed within the context of, and in consort with, your ingredient sourcing, your equipment, your staffing, and your concept.

Sourcing: The array of ingredients that you will need to source and stock are determined by your menu. After you complete a first menu draft, list all ingredients required to prepare every item on your menu and see which ones might be used only once or twice. If that list is long, consider revising your menu to reduce the total number of items you need to stock, which will in turn reduce storage space, shopping time, and food spoilage.

Kitchen equipment: More than any other factor, your menu will dictate the type and range of the commercial kitchen equipment your will require. In most cases, the size, type, and variety of equipment is limited by a number of givens: kitchen size, hood size, electrical capacity of the building, and capacity of gas to the building. Given these limitations, a menu that demands a great variety of equipment many mean that each piece of equipment must be downsized, potentially limiting its capacity. A lean, compact menu helps you achieve a streamlined kitchen with fewer different types of equipment, which can function well and dependably at peak capacity.

Your kitchen design and your menu development must proceed hand-in-hand, as changes in one will result in changes in the other.

Staffing and training: There is a strong link between the items you offer on your menu and how you staff. Certain items require more skill to produce, necessitating a more skilled staff. Ideally, your menu will be developed in consort with your kitchen manager, as you grow and flesh out your restaurant concept, and will respond to, or at least take into account, the skill level of your current and future staff.

Concept: Nowhere is your restaurant concept more evident than in your menu. Solely from the standpoint of your menu, is your concept clear and evident?

Competition: Does your menu offer something different than competitors in your trade area?

Your background and experience: If you are particularly familiar and experienced with the preparation of one style of food, that may become both a driver of your concept and for your menu. Growing up eating a certain cuisine can give you a deep familiarity and a high level of discernment with it.

Though I have cooked all of my adult life, overall I am neither a particularly accomplished nor a refined cook. Growing up in northern New Mexico, and eating and loving the food from there, I invested the effort over decades to learn to cook it well. Opening my first restaurant, it was natural for me to create a concept and then a menu focused on this very spicy, very old cuisine. Fortunately, I'm not the only fan of it.

ATTRIBUTES OF A GOOD MENU

From the customer's standpoint, what makes one menu instantly more appealing, more comfortable, than another? Here are a few general menu attributes that we can look at.

Organization: Consider menu organization from the standpoint of the customer. They should be able to navigate the menu effortlessly, squandering the least amount of time possible going down dead ends (investigating food options that ultimately they will have no interest in) and arrive expeditiously at their goal, finding the dish that most suits their preferences, appetite, and price point.

As an example, visualize two different sandwich menus, each with the same sandwiches. The first menu has a cutesy name for each sandwich, a lengthy description of every ingredient in the sandwich, and no evident organizational structure. Thus the customer must laboriously read through the description of each item in order to evaluate it, and rule it out, or file it away as a possibility to be returned to.

Compare this to a menu where the same sandwiches are first divided by hot or cold, and then are sorted by the dominant protein in each (e.g., pork, chicken, etc.) or lack of animal protein (e.g., vegetarian, vegan, etc.).

This allows the hungry customer to quickly eliminate, without feckless investigation, the vast majority of the menu and to zero in on the selections that are potentially appealing to them. This demands much less from the customer, speeds up the process, and communicates that you value customer-centric organization.

A traditional way of organizing a menu is: specialties/signature dishes, snacks, soups, salads, main dishes, desserts, drinks (non-alcoholic cold drinks first, then hot, then alcoholic). There is some merit in employing this or a similar structure so as to orient the customer and make their navigation easier.

Manageability and simplicity: I've already discussed the implications of menu on the number of ingredients required to be kept on hand, and on kitchen equipment. Additionally, a large menu is difficult for customers to navigate and understand in a short amount of time. Generally it is best to resist the urge to have a great many similar items and, if you err to one side of the other, err on the side of brevity. Having a short menu consisting of several well-considered items communicates that you do a few things very well, rather than that you do a mediocre job of preparing many items. As well, when a restaurant has a ponderous menu, it may raise, in the mind of the customer, the question of the rate of turnover of ingredients and their consequent freshness.

Simplicity should apply to your item descriptions as well. There is a temptation to list each ingredient of a dish, its pedigree or source, and method of preparation. For example, "Hengstenburg Farms baby beets julienned and braised in a Stonewater Creek pinot noir combined with ..." Compare this to "Beets, red wine ..." Most customers much prefer the latter, particularly when trying to take in an entire menu. There is a counter-argument that the consumer places a certain value on an item and that value goes up with each descriptor, that for the consumer, for example, "Hengstenburg Farms baby beets," invokes a greater sense of value than does "beets." I leave it to you to find a middle ground, a sweet spot between being too spare and too verbose in your menu descriptions.

Legibility: It seems obvious that a customer would not want to struggle to read a menu, yet still plenty of menus are executed in ways that make reading them difficult, particularly for older eyes. To make your menu highly legible, keep fonts simple, use ample white space, and make sure the font size is large enough for the distance from which the menu will be read. Avoid a low contrast between the font and the background color. Make sure there is ample illumination in the area where the menu will be read.

Balance: Like a painting, a menu should exhibit balance in its composition. Balance is required in a variety of continuums including:

Heavy vs. light: There should be items that span the range from calorically very dense to very light. Customers should be able to match caloric intensity with their appetites and diets.

Expensive vs. inexpensive and elaborate vs. simple: A menu in which too many of the options require highly complex preparation may bog down the kitchen and frustrate diners looking for something simple and quick. A balanced menu provides offerings at a variety of price points.

Originality vs. predictability: Original recipes help your independent restaurant set itself apart from your competition, and from multi-store chains. However, diners often crave the familiar and predictable. A balanced menu has something to offer both preferences.

Wet vs. dry: This may seem like an odd continuum, but there are times when a diner is in the mood to chew, and might desire something with tooth resistance, say, a cut of meat, and other times when they are craving something with a soft mouthfeel, perhaps a dish smothered in sauce or something otherwise very soft and wet. It is useful to provide both options.

PRICING YOUR MENU ITEMS

On the one hand, your prices must be perceived as logical, fair, and appealing by your customers. On the other hand, they should maximize your profitability. Assigning a price to each menu item is a serious and consequential task.

Like anything else being transacted in an open market, competition and supply and demand are the forces that create acceptable pricing. That being the case, it is important to corral all of the pricing information that you possibly can from competing establishments in your trade area, and in similar trade areas in your market.

COMPETITIVE MARKET ANALYSIS

Try to find the same menu item on as many different competitors' menus as possible, and enter them all into a spreadsheet, identifying the dish, restaurant, and price, and noting any substantial differences that would make one variation have substantially more or less value than another. Using this data, you can identify a price range and, based on the quality of your version, location of your restaurant, and demographics of your customer base, identify an area within the price range for the item that will be perceived by customers as logical and fair for what you are offering.

In Albuquerque, my home city, by far the most popular breakfast item is huevos rancheros, typically two eggs served atop warmed corn tortillas, smothered in red or green chile, and served with hash brown or pan-fried potatoes and a hot flour tortilla and butter. Over the years I have sampled dozens of different competitors' versions of this locally ubiquitous dish, and dutifully entered each into a spreadsheet, noting price, restaurant quality, ingredient quality, etc. This dish is offered by the humblest fast-food carryout eateries to moderately upscale full service restaurants, so the price varies substantially, as does the quality of the ingredients. In doing this what I have strived for is that the price of this dish at Tia Betty's is near the midpoint of the range. While I believe our quality is unsurpassed, we are a counter-service restaurant in a trade area where about half of the residents have a very low household income. This price point seems to work for our customers and for us.

COST RATIO PERCENTAGE PRICING

Identifying a price point indicated by an analysis of your competitors' pricing of similar offerings does not in itself indicate that that price point will be profitable for you, the restaurant owner. To insure that any one dish is profitable, restaurant owners typically employ a cost of food ratio, looking at the price indicated by a multiplier of the direct cost of the food in the item. What multiplier you use will vary depending on the food type, but generally a menu item priced at 300 percent to 400 percent of the direct food costs for the item will be profitable. However, this assumes a normal range of indirect costs (labor, rent, etc.). If those costs are particularly high or low, you may need to adjust your food-cost-to-price ratio accordingly. Customers expect virtually the same item to cost more at a restaurant that provides a higher level of service, paying more for the same item at a full service vs. counter service establishment. The reason for this largely relates to the greater indirect costs (labor, rent, etc.) associated with restaurants providing a higher level of service.

GROSS PROFIT METHOD

One issue with the cost multiplier method of pricing is that the percentage multiplier you use, at your particular sales volume, and with your particular cost structure, may not actually be sufficient to ensure profitability. Without further information and analysis there is no way for you to know that pricing a dish at three or four times the cost of ingredients will actually result in a net profit. Using the cost multiplier method, even if the multiplier you are using does result in a profit, the profit will not be the same for each item. That is, it will be a percentage of the sales price rather than an absolute amount per item, which may not be ideal.

The gross profit method of pricing is used to achieve a uniform absolute amount of net profit per item sold, based on your exact cost structure. This is done by determining how much gross profit you need per item sold, other than the product cost of the item, to cover your operating costs and a predetermined amount of annual profit based on prior year, or on projected future, unit sales.

To calculate a price using the gross profit method, it is helpful if you have your operating costs and sales data from the last prior year or, in the case of a new restaurant, you can substitute an accurate projection of costs for the first year of operation.

Begin by totaling all of the costs of operating your restaurant, excluding your product or ingredient costs (we will deal with that later). To your total operating costs, add your profit target (likely 10 percent to 20 percent of gross sales). This gives you your accumulated annual gross profit, an total amount sufficient to cover your operating expenses (not including cost of food) and a built-in annual profit.

This number then needs to be divided into sales categories based on the percentage of your prior year, or anticipated, gross sales for each category (e.g., entrees, beverages, alcohol, etc.). You can then determine an accumulated annual gross profit for each category.

Next you will determine the number of items sold per category, for instance, how many total entrees, how many total alcoholic drinks, etc. Once you know the total items sold or anticipated to be sold in each category annually, you can divide the annual gross profit attributed to that category by the number of items sold annually in that category to determine a gross profit per item needed.

LET'S WALK THROUGH AN EXAMPLE:

A restaurant had $1,000,000 in gross sales last year and total operating costs of $700,000, of which product costs (food costs or costs of products sold, beverages, alcohol, etc.) were $300,000. Assume the owner had a target profit of 15 percent of gross sales, or $150,000. The owner wishes to price an entrée item. Entrées accounted for 50 percent of total sales last year and 25,000 individual entrées were sold. The cost of food for the menu item in question is $3.

1. First we must determine our annual Accumulated Gross Profit. This is equal to the total annual operating expenses excluding the product costs (the ingredient or food cost for each item) plus target annual profit.

   (All Annual Expenses - Product Cost) + Annual Profit Target = Accumulated Gross Profit

   ($700,000 - $300,000) + $150,000 = $550,000

2. Next, we allocate the percentage of our accumulated gross profit to the area of sales we are examining, in this case entrées. Fifty percent of last year's sales were from entrees, so $550,000 (50 percent) = $225,000. So, $225,000 of Accumulated Gross Profit is allocated to the entrée category.

3. Or sales records from last year tell us that we sold 25,000 entrées last year. To determine the amount we must charge for each entrée item (not including product cost), we divide last year's sales in that category by the number of sales. Gross sales in category ÷ items sold = sales price per item required to generate accumulated gross profit in this category (not including food cost)

   $225,000 ÷ 25,000 = $9

4. This tells us that we must charge $9 for every entrée item in addition to the cost of food, in this case $3. The price we must charge for this particular entrée item is $12 in order to hit our target annual profit. $9 + $3 = $12

This process can be repeated for every category of item on your menu. Assuming your sales volume stays consistent or improves, and that you make periodic adjustments to reflect changes in operating costs and food costs, you should hit your target annual profit. Obviously, this method of pricing is only as accurate as your prior year sales data, or projected sales, that you base it on, so it will have more utility after you achieve stabilized sales.

YOUR MENU'S APPEARANCE

Aside from its primary purpose, efficiently conveying essential information to your customers, you menu is a piece of graphic design unto itself. A poorly designed, aesthetically unappealing menu can undermine your customer's confidence in your food, attention to detail, and craft before they even place their order.

There is a way of viewing competence in any area of endeavor that is worth mentioning. If we divide levels of competence into four stages of mastery, the starting point, stage one, is the period where we know so little about something that we have no idea that we know nothing about it. As we progress to the second stage of mastery, we acquire a beginner's level of knowledge, and with that become aware that we actually have very little competence in that given area and much to learn. As our competence grows we enter stage three, where we poses some true skill and competence but lack mastery. Finally, in stage four we achieve some level of mastery in the field. All of us have areas in our life wherein our competence is at stage one. Having competence level in stage one can be very dangerous if that area is a very public one, because we honestly don't know that we don't know what we are doing, but our incompetence will be painfully obvious to other people.

I have seen a number of independent restaurant menu designs that clearly were designed by someone who was either at stage one in their level of competence in graphic design and had no idea how awful their menu looked, or maybe was at some higher level of competence and just didn't think it mattered. Either way, the result was to unnecessarily make a bad impression on a great many customers before they even ordered.

If you have some background, skill, and natural talent for graphic composition, and familiarity with any of the popular graphic art programs, you may be able to produce a very appealing menu that is graphically clear, not overly busy, and is both pleasing to the eye and easy for the customer to navigate. This is a great skill set to have, as it makes modifications to your menus fast and simple. However, if graphic design is new to you, you may be better off hiring a graphic designer to compete your design. Or, you may wish to hire a designer to create an initial template for you that you can modify yourself over time as your menu changes.

If you are designing your own menu, avoid the temptation to use a many different fonts, an entire bouquet colors, and a parade of different font sizes. Simpler is better!

I design all of my own menus and learned a simple trick a few years ago that has made the task much easier and drastically improved the quality of the finished product. It has to do with the colors I use in the menu. There are a number of books you can purchase that have entire pallets of three, four, or five color schemes, assembled by contributing artists such that grouping of colors' tones, hues, and intensities all work together harmoniously. Some of these books include a DVD that contains each palette as a standalone .jpg file. This allows you, once you select a color palette for your menu, to import it into whatever graphic design software you are using, and then to color your background, headline, or text fonts to match the colors in the imported palette without spending endless hours refining the exact colors for compatibility. This works wonderfully to give your menu a very refined, fine-tuned color composition that would otherwise elude most of us.

Another option is to use a menu template. There are many available online at little or no cost.

Graphically and visually, your menu is a great opportunity to express and reinforce your concept. At Tia Betty's we have inserted into our main wall menus several retro, black-and-white photographic images. They have nothing directly to do with the food, but I believe that they clearly reinforce many aspects of the restaurant concept. The photos are from the 1940s and 1950s, a key piece of our feel, and they depict mostly smiling everyday people enjoying their food.

In addition to being well organized, your menu should advance your marketing goals. In many cases, some of your menu items will earn a greater net profit than others, and it makes sense to list these items near the top in each category. As well, you can use color, photos, or boxes to highlight items you particularly to draw attention to them.

You may wish to consider including photos of some food items. Photos of every item may make the entire menu look busy and difficult to approach. Never use a photo unless it is of such quality, and will reproduce at such a quality, that it actually improves one's sense of the dish beyond what the consumer might have imagined based on a simple description. If the photo does not make the dish look appetizing, don't use it. No photo is far better than a bad photo. A good photo may be particularly useful when the dish is largely unfamiliar to diners. Few people want to risk ordering something that they can't visualize.

Resources: How to Write Great Restaurant Menu Descriptions by Steve Bareham

Eight

Site selection – finding the perfect location for your restaurant

L ikely the single most consequential decision you will make in the process of establishing your restaurant is the selection of a site or location. Selecting the right location will enable you to attract a high number of your ideal potential customers and create a good fit in all ways between what your restaurant offers and what the potential customers in the surrounding trade area want. Making a poor decision in site selection portends insufficient customers, less-than-ideal customers, and a poor fit between your concept and the pool of restaurant patrons in the surrounding area. Selecting the right site provides the opportunity for you to leverage, or receive maximal return on, all of your future time and money investment. Selecting a poor location may not always doom your enterprise, but it will guarantee that many things – attracting the best customers and creating return customers – will be more difficult and more costly than would otherwise be the case. And, unlike errors you might make in other areas of your restaurant – for instance, in some aspect of your concept, or in developing your menu, or in selecting equipment – you cannot easily remedy the error by changing your location once you have opened your restaurant there.

MOVING FROM A MARKET OVERVIEW TOWARD POTENTIAL TRADE AREAS

Once you have researched and clearly articulated your restaurant concept, you can begin the site selection process. Start by considering the
demographics characteristics (ethnicity, age, income, education, etc.) and
psychographic groups (population segments described by behaviors)
that will be most attracted to and supportive of your concept. With a clear
sense of the demographic characteristics and psychographic groups that
you are seeking, you can then locate areas and pockets in your market
rich in people with these characteristics.

Before considering specific trade areas, take some time to acquire
an overview of the distribution of various different demographic variable
throughout your entire city, or market area. Using either a third-party demographic data provider (see resources list at the end of this chapter) or
the services of a commercial real estate broker with access to the same
data, create themed maps of your entire market area, using color to represent only one demographic variable. For instance, you might create a
household income themed map where lower income areas are indicated
in cooler-toned colors that transition to warmer tones as household income increases. You might also do the same with average age, or any
other variable particularly relevant to your concept. Creating a number of
themed maps of your entire market, each reflecting the transition of one
variable, you can quickly identify areas and pockets that appear promising, you will want to look at more closely, as well as entire areas you may
want to discard.

You can then work to locate specific sites roughly in these promising
areas With each prospective site as the center point, evaluate potential
surrounding trade areas, the geographically defined area surrounding each site that will account for the vast majority of your restaurant's

business at that location. If the trade area is satisfactory, indicating that there is sufficient available potential business at that location to support your restaurant, you can move forward with evaluating the specific aspects of each site and building.

This is the typical process because most restaurants are clones, part of a chain, and the owner is seeking to replicate the conditions (trade area) surrounding their most successful restaurants in the chain, to duplicate its success. However, the site selection process can also work in reverse, beginning with a prospective site or property. Based on an analysis of the trade area surrounding it, you could also develop a concept specifically designed to thrive in that location.

WHAT IS A TRADE AREA AND WHY IS IT SO IMPORTANT?

Your trade area is the specific geographic area surrounding your restaurant which, by definition, will be the origin of at least 70 percent of your restaurant's business. If you imagine your restaurant as the center point of a circle, your trade area might very roughly be a circle of sufficient size such that it captures the geographic area where at least 70 percent of your potential customers either live or work.

Underlying the concept of a trade area is the understanding that most people prefer to travel the shortest distance possible to make a purchase or eat a meal. Thus the proximity of your restaurant to the potential customer is a major determinant as to whether or not the potential customer can be converted to an actual customer, particularly a regular one. Seen another way, since proximity is such a big factor in how customers select restaurants that it makes sense to thoroughly know and understand those potential customers who live or work close enough to a potential site to make sure that there are enough of them, and that they have the means, tastes, and preferences to become regular customers.

The precise boundaries, and therefore the size or area, of a trade area surrounding a planned restaurant are not easy to accurately determine (it is easier once your restaurant is established, because you can track customers using identifying data such as address or zip code). The density of the population in the trade area, of both residents and workers, and the number and exact location of competitors, will impact the size and shape of your trade area. In most urban and suburban settings the majority of your customers will come from a distance of a mile or less, but in less densely populated areas customers may come from several miles. Also, in reality, trade areas are rarely perfect circles. Difficult-to-cross boundaries such as rivers, freeways, or even undesirable areas that customers may hesitate to walk through, and differing levels of density, all work together to form polygon or amoeba-shaped trade areas.

Initially, for simplicity, you can plot various-sized boundaries of a potential trade area using a circle (which represents people traveling equally from all directions to arrive at your restaurant) or, to model different potential sizes of a trade area, concentric circles. Your restaurant site will be the center point of the circle or circles. Though the size of each concentric ring, its radius will vary depending on population density (smaller for a densely populated urban area, larger for a less-populated suburban area), a typical range of restaurant trade areas are thought of as having a 0.5-mile, 1-mile, and 2-mile radius. It may be more helpful, depending on the dynamics of your exact area, to measure distance in driving or walking time.

Even though defining a trade area for a yet-to-be-built restaurant is imprecise, given the number of unknown variable (popularity, singularity of food, impact of competitors, etc.), it is still one of the most important things you can do to select a winning location.

Consider this metaphor: you would likely not transplant a rare and expensive botanical specimen into your garden without knowing its requirements for soil, climate, and water. Similarly, you should define the boundaries of, analyze, and understand a given trade area before you can know if it will support your restaurant concept.

Within half a mile of my house are two very high-quality fast-casual breakfast/lunch restaurants. Both have appealing atmospheres, great service, and neither has ever disappointed me with the quality and appeal of its food. One is thriving, consistently operating at or near capacity. On weekends there will seldom be a vacant seat and there is often a wait for a table. The other, smaller, restaurant, rarely has more than a third of its seats occupied and I have never once seen it operating at anywhere near capacity. It keeps its doors open but hardly seems profitable. What is the big difference between these two similar restaurants?

If you were to draw a circle around each on a map with a half-mile radius, the differences in trade areas quickly becomes evident. The entire mile-wide ring surrounding the first restaurant, the one that is always busy, is filled with single-family residences, mostly having both household incomes and a median age that are substantially higher than average for our city. There would be a few pockets of daytime employees in the circle, and none of them would be cut off from the restaurant by physical barrier, allowing employees to easily walk to and from this restaurant over lunch hour.

The second restaurant borders a wide and busy street and the area extending in one direction beyond that street is a railroad track, which only has a few widely separated crossing points. Beyond the railroad tracks are office buildings that are totally vacant during the evenings and weekends. Due to a combination of a physical barrier and offices that are vacant over the weekend, it is as though the second restaurant has an actual trade area in the shape of a semi-circle, with the restaurant situated at the center of the flat side. The trade area if the second restaurant is effectively half the size of that of the first restaurant. Contemplating these two restaurants, both lovely and enviable in every other way, one thriving and one perpetually operating at a fraction of its capacity, it is evident how critical it is *that you study trade areas before committing to a location for your restaurant. To use our horticultural metaphor, no matter the plant's inherent potential, it won't thrive in poor soil.*

EVALUATING THE TRADE AREA SURROUNDING A SITE

After you have identified general areas in your market in which you would consider locating, that have overall demographics that appear promising for your restaurant, and then have located possible available locations within those areas, you can begin gathering data about each site, each site's trade area, and the demographics and psychographics specific to each trade area.

If the property is listed for sale or lease by a commercial real estate broker, an information package for the property should be readily available and should include: a site plan showing the building as it sits on the site (helpful to understand parking, ingress and egress, potential outdoor seating, etc. ...), a floor plan indicating the building square footage, and basic demographics for the surrounding 1-mile, 3-mile, and 5-mile diameter rings and some aerial or bird's eye view image that will allow you to understand the immediately surrounding built environment. The package should indicate, in the event of a lease, both the asking rent and the proposed lease structure, and the proposed lease term.

In analyzing the demographics and psychographics in the potential trade area, you will be looking for a population rich in potential ideal customers for your restaurant concept. What age group is most likely to patronize your restaurant as defined by age, income, net worth, education, and family size? What segmented psychographic groups are more likely to patronize restaurants in general and yours in particular?

The best trade areas align with your restaurant concept's core consumer profile and also have the right density of residential, employment, and retail establishments to support a sales volume sufficient for the restaurant to thrive.

In evaluating a trade area surrounding a site, here are some of the key demographic variables:

Population density: In comparing trade areas, denser is almost always better, all other factors being equal. Why? Because greater density of population means that within a given geographic area, say a 1- or 2-mile radius of your site, or a five-minute drive time, you will have more potential customers than a similar-sized less-dense area. Conversely, a low density of residents or daytime workers means that within a reasonably sized geographic trade area there may not be enough potential customers to support your business or that potential customers will be coming from further away, which will likely reduce the frequency of their visits to your restaurant.

Daytime work population: A population does not necessarily need to reside in your trade area to become your customers. Some trade areas contain few "rooftops" (residential homes), but do have a large daytime work population. This can function in lieu of a residential base in your market area, or it supplement it. Having both a dense residential base and a weekday daytime work population can also be a fantastic mix, allowing a restaurant to do a vibrant weekday breakfast and lunch business catering to the daytime work population and a strong evening and or weekend business catering to the residents. If daytime workers are a significant part of your target demographic, make sure that there are no geographic barriers to them quickly reaching your restaurant and that your concept incorporates fast service.

Affluence: The level of affluence in trade areas can be measured by the average net worth, or per capita income, or household income of the residents. Conventional wisdom is that the more affluent a neighborhood is, the higher the average household earnings, the more desirable the demographic for a restaurant. The idea is that the higher the income the greater the level of disposable income, the greater the ability of residents to dine out. While there is logic to this, in most cases I think it is better to take a more nuanced approach and look at the potential fit for your concept with the complex demographic and psychographic makeup of the trade area, rather than to simply focus on the resident's level of earnings. There are restaurants that exclusively select trade areas for new stores with very low household earnings because the restaurants price point is very low, and they have fine-tuned their concept to do well in low-income and often under-served areas. As is the case with so many other demographic variables, the goal is a happy marriage between your concept and the customers in your trade area.

Education: For some restaurant concepts, educational attainment – the average level of education of the residents of the surrounding trade area – is more predictive of success or failure than the resident's level of income or net worth. Two decades ago the Boulder, CO-based grocery chain Wild Oats (now Whole Foods) began using educational attainment as one of its primary demographic variables in site selection, realizing that it was more predictive of potential customers predisposed to patronize their stores than income data was. I suspect many coffee shops and hip eateries would find the same to be the case.

Ethnicity: People's culture and ethnicity manifests in their choice of restaurants. On an obvious level, if your food is of, and designed to appeal to, a particular ethnicity, you would likely seek a trade area with a high concentration of people of that ethnicity. On a more subtle level, certain ethnic groups may account for a larger percentage of sales at a given restaurant than the percentage of the surrounding population that they account for (e.g., a certain ethnicity accounts for 10 percent of the population in a certain trade area but accounts for 25 percent of the sales at a specific type or style of restaurant in that same area). This phenomenon is called "over index." Many chains are familiar with it and incorporate it into their site selection process. So, if your research indicates that restaurants with a similar concept to yours are "over index" for a given ethnicity, seek trade areas with a greater concentration of people of that ethnicity.

Psychographic fit: Psychographics separate populations into segments based primarily on the point that they are at in their life cycles, their affluence, and their collective behavior. Often behaviors (What are their values? What sort of car do they drive?) are much better, more useful, and more accurate predictors of consumer preferences than is purely demographic information. It is well worth becoming familiar with the primary psychographic segmentation system used in the U.S.: Nielsen PRIZM (formerly Claritas Prizm), which segments and groups are most likely to be attracted to your concept, and then seek out trade areas rich in these groups. At the end of this chapter we will discuss options for accessing both demographic and psychographic information. In the segmentation appendix I have included an organizational chart and description of each of the 64 PRIZM segments.

Aside from demographics and psychographics, what are the things we can look for in choosing between competing trade areas?

Traffic generators: More people entering a trade area means more customers. For this reason other destinations within your trade area, particularly those attracting people likely to become customers, have great value. Desirable traffic generators include movie theatres, shopping complexes, hospitals, and tourist attractions. All other factors being equal, a trade area with significant traffic generators is more desirable than one without them.

Competitors: Any given market area will have a certain level of demand for restaurants of various types, and that demand is then satisfied between your restaurant and competing ones. Ideally you would be able to identify some level of unmet or pent-up, demand, but this is rare. More often your business will come at the expense of existing competitors.

You can evaluate the negative impact of competitors based on two continuums: proximity and similarity. The further away a competitor is from our site, the less its potential impact. Expressed another way, the smaller the overlap between your and a competitor's trade area, the less its impact on your business. The more similar a competing restaurant in your trade area is in its concept, hours of operation, appeal to a particular market segment, and price point, the greater the potential that you will be splitting available business with it. Although an area might initially seem dense with competitors, look more closely at their operation and concept before deciding you will be competing for the same customers.

The trade area surrounding my restaurant, Tia Betty's, is chock-full of other restaurants catering to daytime workers, those working at the adjacent hospitals, labs, and the air force base. Initially this gave me some concern in selecting the location, but after inventory-ing each of them, I realized that all except one were chain and franchise establishments and that one was of an ethnic food unrelated to my concept. I realized that although the trade area was crowded with restaurants, due to the lack of similarity between the existing restaurants and my planned restaurant, I would likely have little meaningful competition and so went forward with the location.

Walkability: Walkability is the degree to which an area is friendly to the presence of people living, shopping, visiting, or spending time there based on how amenable it is to walking. Factors influencing walkability include the presence or absence of footpaths, sidewalks, or other pedestrian rights-of-way, traffic and road conditions, land use patterns, building accessibility, and safety.

If you are considering a potential site where you anticipate that a great deal of the traffic will be from foot traffic, it is important to take into account the varying degrees of walkability from one neighborhood to the next. Factors that contribute to a high degree of walkability are:

residential density, presence of trees and vegetation, and transparency (being able to see into buildings as you walk by them).

There is a proprietary system for evaluating an area's relative walkability and assigning it a score. Although this system is not exactly fine-tuned to the considerations of restaurant customers, it is still a simple (and free!) way to get a quick read on the relative walkability of competing sites. Visit walkscore.com, enter the addresses of potential sites you are considering, and see the walk score it generates.

Area charm and character: An area's inherent visual interest, charm, and character can be heavily correlated with its walkability, since people love to walk in pleasant, interesting, and bustling areas, but a neighborhood's charm and character goes beyond walkability. These qualities can be the result of historic architecture, urban redevelopment, public art, or open-air cafes. Being located in an area that people enjoy exploring and hanging out in and find charming can be a boon to a restaurant and can tip the scales in favor of one location over another.

Adjacencies: Adjacencies refer to nearby businesses that may impact the appeal of your business. Obviously, avoid locating your restaurant next to any source of odor such as a pet store or beauty salon. Adjacent businesses with a positive impact might include foot-traffic generators such as anchor tenants in a retail center or nearby entertainment related venues.

Barriers: There are a variety of types of physical and psychological barriers that can impede access to your potential restaurant. Physical barriers most often involve difficulties with driving or walking to your site such as a river, freeway, or other features of the landscape that prevents easy access.

Psychological barriers are any combination of factors that serve to inhibit a potential customer from frequenting the area. This might be a marked reduction in the perceived safety of an area, a sudden reduction in lighting, or a noticeable change in the character of the businesses (like a change from mostly small retail buildings to large office buildings). Any condition that would cause the customer to feel unsafe or uncomfortable, say, having to walk by a busy bar with drunk patrons spilling out into the street, may pose a psychological barrier and will serve to dissuade some amount of business.

In my hometown of Albuquerque a few years ago, I noticed a building that housed a low-end breakfast dive restaurant changed hands. The new owners completed a lovely remodel and opened what quickly became regarded as the best upscale seafood restaurant in town. The site was a mere quarter-mile from our city's most vibrant, revitalized, and walkable restaurant and retail hub, Nob Hill. However, I think that quarter-mile proved deadly. It was an unappealing stretch of no-man's-land inhabited by low-end retail and several adult entertainment establishments. It was clear that there was a huge psychological barrier between the vibrant restaurant hub of Nob Hill and this island of a restaurant. In practical terms, a potential patron parked in Nob Hill, considering several restaurants and their wait times, would be highly unlikely to walk the quarter mile, at night, through an unsavory and unappealing area to try out a wonderful new restaurant. I suspect many were even concerned with their safety parking in the facilities parking lot and walking in to the restaurant. The restaurant failed in about a year and now, several years later, the beautifully remodeled space is sitting empty, on the market. Beware any barriers between your site and your customers, be they physical or psychological.

Captive consumers: A captive consumer is one who has few food options, such as with restaurants in airports, office buildings, and isolated underserved areas. The advantages of trade area that contains some element of captive consumers are a lack of competition.

Crime: Crime statistics are available online through the graphic information system (GIS) portion of many cities' municipal websites. As well, most packages of demographic information will include crime statistics. Obviously, less crime relative to your city's average is better. A high crime rate can act as a psychological barrier for your prospective customers.

HOW DOES A PROSPECTIVE SITE FUNCTION WITH ITS SURROUNDING NEIGHBORHOOD?

After evaluating the overall trade area, you can turn your attention to other characteristics of the neighborhood around the prospective site, and examine how the site might function as a restaurant in the context of the existing neighborhood.

Vehicular accessibility: The most well-located and highly-visible site will still underperform if your customers cannot easily access it. In most cases this means vehicular access. If the property is located on a busy corridor, is there a turn lane such that traffic on the opposite side of street can turn in rather than having to make a U-turn or having to circle around the block? Once a customer reaches the property, are there ample curb cuts to allow easy ingress to and egress from surrounding streets? Does traffic back up behind curb cuts, impinging egress or access onto the site? On your initial and subsequent site inspections, take note of the ease of vehicular site access.

Traffic: In general, more traffic is better than less traffic, as more traffic means more people are being exposed to your restaurant. However, greater traffic volume will likely only translate into more customers if other conditions are present such as ample parking, good site access, and a speed limit slow enough to permit potential customers enough time to take note of your business and to make a timely decision as to whether to stop. Vehicular traffic volume is typically expressed as the average annual daily traffic (AADT), which is the total annual volume of traffic for a roadway divided by 365. In most municipalities information regarding AADT is readily available online for every major street. However, for most restaurant owners, average daily traffic is much less relevant than traffic at peak times, typically breakfast, lunch, and dinner. To get a handle on the rise and fall of traffic during different times of day, you may actually have to park and count cars for yourself. Knowing when peak traffic volumes occur, how large they are, and when and to what degree they fall off, can be extraordinarily useful in your site selection.

Take note of the speed limit of the street fronting the property. A higher speed limit means less time for the potential customer to view your signage and take in the presence of your restaurant, while a slower speed limit gives them time to note and consider your business.

Site visibility: Clearly, there is a connection between potential customers ability to see your premises, there awareness of it, and their willingness to try it. If a person is unaware of your business, they can't try it. Visibility is a huge advantage, taking the place of and or leveraging your other advertising efforts.

The distance your building is set back from the street is a consideration. The greater the setback from the street, generally, the less the visibility of your building to passersby and the greater the likelihood that surrounding buildings will hide it. Having a view corridor – is being able to see your site or building from a distance, unobstructed by surrounding buildings – is important for site visibility.

Trees, either along a street or in a setback area, can limit visibility, although may ultimately redeem themselves and prove to be a net asset in the character, sense of place, and shade they provide. Site grade can impact visibility. If the dominant grade is below the street or drops off toward the back of the site, your building may be largely hidden.

When evaluating space in a multi-tenant strip center, consider the orientation of the center relative to the primary street fronting it. Strip centers that are positioned perpendicular to a major street, rather than parallel to it, generally have very low visibility. Endcaps of strip centers typically have much greater visibility than do the inline spaces in the same center.

Side of street: If a street is heavily used by commuters to reach their workplace there will naturally be an increase in traffic going one direction for the morning commute and the other direction for their going-home drive. This, combined with the ease of making a right-hand turn into a business, compared with the relative difficulty of making a left-hand turn across traffic into the same business, can substantially impact a restaurant's business at the busiest times of the day. A restaurant offering drive-through coffee and breakfast items will do best on the "morning" side of the street (the side used by commuters to go to work), and a restaurant offering take away diners would do best on the "going home" side of the street.

Synergy: It is worth contemplating which potential neighboring businesses might function synergistically with your restaurant. Businesses that encourage people to walk about, art galleries, boutique clothing shops, and bookstores can work to form a nice synergy with outdoor cafes, gelato shops, coffee shops, and the like.

IS THE SITE WELL SUITED FOR A RESTAURANT?
Now let's change our focus from looking at how the site functions with its surroundings to examining the qualities of the site itself.

Zoning: It is imperative that the existing zoning for any potential site allow for your intended use or that you are willing to shoulder the burden in cost, time, and energy involved in attempting to change it and to accept the risk of an uncertain outcome. Even if the existing zoning allows for use of the property as a restaurant, it can still limit your business by what specifics it allows, for example: whether a drive-through window will be permitted, whether a change to the building exterior or appearance is allowed, whether alcohol sales will be allowed, what the required amount of parking is, and what type and amount of signage is allowed. It is best to approach zoning from two angles. First, familiarize yourself with the general zoning classifications in your municipality that allow for restaurants so that you can focus your search on properties with that zoning. Second, investigate the exact details of the zoning of each proposed site. Often in the case of redeveloped historical areas, there will be zoning that is very specific to that area, and it is essential that you completely understand it and all restrictions it imposes.

Parking: Restaurants are parking hogs. Ideally, unless you expect lots of pedestrian traffic, there should be 15 to 20 parking spaces available per 1,000 square feet of building space, unless you expect lots of pedestrian traffic. Parking requirements need to be met on two levels: conformity to applicable zoning regulations and convenience for your customers. Before you begin inspections of prospective sites, acquaint yourself with the parking requirements imposed by local zoning ordinances for restaurants. These vary with each municipality, but typically range from 10 to 13 spaces per 1,000 square feet of building space. This is particularly essential when you are considering changing the use of an existing building that has not previously been used as a restaurant to a restaurant use, as you will likely be required to meet current-year zoning and building code and regulations, with no allowance for "grandfathered-in" conditions.

From a customer accommodation standpoint, it may be possible to offset a lack of on-site parking when there is ample available street parking, or a nearby public parking facility. As well, some locations have high levels of foot traffic, which might offset much of your parking requirement. However, a significant insufficiency of parking, even if allowed by your municipal governmental authorities, may dissuade some percentage of would-be patrons and can act as a permeant drag on your business, forever weighing down and reducing the effectiveness of all of your marketing efforts.

When considering space in a multi-tenant retail facility with shared parking, determining adequacy of parking can be more complex. Parking availability may fluctuate seasonally, and throughout the day, depending on the business patterns of the other tenants. Will any of the other tenants place a large demand on parking at the same time of day that your restaurant will be experiencing its peak business?

Gyms located in the same retail center as your restaurant can be a problem, having large parking requirements that peak early in the morning and early in the evening, likely at the same times as your restaurant's breakfast and dinner peak business hours. Bars and nightclubs can also be evening parking hogs.

Signage: In evaluating a potential site, signage is mostly evaluated from the standpoint of any limitations imposed on it. Sites with fewer restrictions on signage are almost always preferable to those with more limitations. Restrictions on signage are imposed in three ways; regulatory, landlord, and practical. Zoning ordinances will typically include regulations regarding the total combined square footage of signage (typically through a formula that takes into account the amount and type of street frontage), the allowable sign type (freestanding vs. flush mounted on the building) and the maximum size. Building owners may institute their own signage rules, governing size and appearance, particularly in the case of multi-tenant retail centers. Aside from governmental and building owner-imposed rules, there is the matter of practicality. How much exterior surface is there on which to display a sign? Would building signage reduce the visual corridor for your location?

In considering older properties, pay attention to ones with existing, often original, freestanding signs. Often they may be of a size, height, or configuration that is no longer permitted. But because the sign may have been built when it was allowable under the then zoning, it may be deemed "grandfathered in" and allowed to remain and be reused. These older signs can give a new restaurant a huge advantage over competitor's newer signs, which to conform to current zoning. For instance, they may be flush-mounted rather than freestanding.

IS THE BUILDING SUITABLE FOR RESTAURANT USE?

Now let's look at the building itself, with an eye toward determine how amenable it is for use as a restaurant.

Building size: Finding a facility that is the correct size for the amount of business you can reasonably expect, based on your concept and analysis of the surrounding trade area, is crucial. If, for instance, you purchase or lease a facility that has twice as much square footage as you will need, not only will the place feel cavernous and vacant much of the time, but also you will be paying twice the amount of rent or mortgage payment that you need to, likely making your rent-to-gross-sales ratio very poor and probably unsustainable. On the other hand, too small of a facility may fail to fully capture potential available business and worse yet, may not allow you to reach the minimum gross sales required for your restaurant's sustainability. You can establish a preliminary size range based on similar concept restaurants in similar trade areas. Once you advance to the point of evaluating particular buildings, you can do a study of competitors in the proposed trade area to determine potential gross income for your restaurant based on the existing level of restaurant dollars being spent in the same trade area (covered in the chapter on determining profitability). With this information in hand you can calculate the number of seats you will need based on a reasonable rate of table turnover for your restaurant type, and your menu pricing, to back into a more precise acceptable size range.

Prior restaurant use: If the last prior use of your potential location was as a restaurant, congratulations! You may have just saved tens, or hundreds of thousands of dollars. Typically if a building has received approval, and a certificate of occupancy, for restaurant use, that use will be allowed again without your having to submitting plans for a change of use, as long as there was no different, intervening use, between the restaurant uses. As well, it is likely that if the last prior user of the space or building was a restaurant, the current use as a restaurant will be allowed per local zoning ordinance. However, never take that as a given. Always get a zoning inspection prior to committing to buy or lease.

If the general layout of the kitchen, and the overall restaurant floor plan, will work with your concept as is, you may again save thousands of dollars in architectural fees, permitting fees, and construction.

However, even if there was a restaurant in the space previously, the kitchen layout, equipment, and in fact the entire floor plan of the building may not be suitable for your concept. In this case you will absolutely want to know what is possible regarding the modification of the building and how much it will cost. Make any lease or purchase negotiations contingent upon this estimate. Restaurant and commercial kitchen remodels are often more expensive than would first seem the case.

Depth vs. frontage ratio: This ratio expresses the amount of street, or sidewalk, frontage a building has relative to its depth. Clearly the more frontage the more exposure and, conversely, a space that is perpendicular to the street and is long and narrow will be unappealing and, from a space utilization perspective, inefficient. A depth to frontage ratio of 1:3 is thought to be ideal so, for example, a space with 7,500 square feet of area, with this ratio, would have 50 feet of sidewalk frontage and 150 feet of depth.

Drive through window: This feature may range from essential to irrelevant for your concept. As a commercial realtor representing restaurant owners in site selection, I have had several who would not consider any facility without a drive-through window or the potential to add one and, on the other hand, for any sort of fine-dining concept, a drive through window would be irrelevant.

If a drive-through is part of your plan, and a facility does not have one, first verify that the property's zoning allows for it. Many zoning ordinances that permit restaurants do not automatically permit drive through windows. Also, know that to add one you will likely need to commission a study from a traffic engineer to demonstrate that the change is safe from a traffic perspective. Of particular concern is stacking, the possibility that cars waiting in line will extend into an adjacent street and obstruct traffic.

Windows: Windows serve a number of functions for a restaurant. In addition to providing natural light, they provide transparency, allowing would be patrons to see in, projecting an inviting sense of a vibrant and pleasant restaurant interior to people walking and driving by. Windows are expensive to add or modify and thus can be an important consideration as to the suitability of a given space for your restaurant. An abundance of outdoor, or patio, seating can help compensate for a lack of windows. Passersby may not be able to see into your restaurant, but from the tables, umbrellas, and diners on the patio, they get that it is a busy and happening eatery.

Electrical and gas capacity of building: Compare the electrical capacity (the total amps available at the service) of the building with that that will be required by the total load from all of your electrical equipment. If you will be using any heavy electrical equipment that requires three-phase power to operate, make sure that this is available in the building as well. Adding additional electrical service to a building can be expensive, requiring an engineer, design, plan approval, and permitting.

Add up the BTU requirements for all of your equipment plus the heating system, if it is gas. Provide the total BTU requirement to either your gas-certified plumber or mechanical engineer to calculate if the existing gas meter and piping are sufficient to deliver the amount of natural gas you require for your total BTU load.

Outdoor seating potential: If you are in a climate that offers comfortable weather for a significant portion of the year, outdoor seating can be a draw for many diners. As well, for the restaurant owner, outdoor seating can significantly expand the seating capacity of the building, in some cases doubling it. And adding outdoor seating can be done at a nominal cost. If a site has the potential for outdoor seating that is reasonably connected to the structure so that it can be serviced, it can be a huge advantage. Outdoor seating areas can easily be made "dog-friendly" by providing tie-downs for leashes near to some tables and a source of water. If your restaurant will be located in a highly walkable area, having a dog-friendly patio can be a significant competitive advantage.

Curb appeal: Curb appeal, the immediate visual appeal of a property from the street, can be a major consideration in selecting a site. An interesting or historical building can provide an immediate positive image for your restaurant and get it noticed. An ungainly, uninteresting, or dilapidated building may serve to permanently dampen interest in and enthusiasm for your restaurant. Paying a little more for a building with an appealing exterior may be justified as an advertising expense, if you are able to reduce your advertising budget by that same amount.

BEGINNING FROM A SPECIFIC SITE

There are times when the idea for a restaurant begins with a specific site rather than with a restaurant concept. Why would you do this? Perhaps you already own a building and wish to explore developing a restaurant in it or perhaps a given location appeals to you for other reasons – it may be close to your home, or located in an exciting and revitalizing area. Or perhaps an opportunity presents itself, a building turns up on the market that is available at a great price, or lease rate, and you wish to explore the possibility of opening a restaurant in it.

Most likely, for someone opening their first restaurant, there will be elements of each process. You might have a generalized concept and evaluate trade areas and sites in terms of how well they will support it, and then, in response to that site, you might modify your concept to best fit the needs and preferences of the exact customers in the surrounding trade area.

USING A COMMERCIAL REAL ESTATE BROKER ... OR NOT

Having practiced commercial real estate for nearly 30 years, I have a bias. I believe that utilizing the services of a commercial real estate agent, particularly a skilled and experienced one whose primary expertise is in site selection, can be a huge advantage as you consider a location for your restaurant. That said, there are plusses and minuses to committing to and working exclusively with only one agent.

If you decide to engage a commercial real estate broker to represent you, invest some time in interviewing and selecting them. Only select among exclusively commercial real estate agents. Do not use an agent who primarily works in the area of residential sales. The skill set required for each area is completely different, with very little overlap between the two. In selecting a commercial agent, look for years of experience and advanced training in retail real estate and, if possible, specifically in site selection for restaurants. Evidence of advanced training might include either the CCIM or SIOR designations, each conferred by national commercial real estate associations and attesting to years of experience and training.

If you select a commercial real estate broker who have the letters CCIM after their name (a designation conferred by the National Association of

Realtors indicating both educational attainment and experience in commercial real estate that only about 5 percent of commercial realtors earn), they will have access to both demographic and psychographic data as part of the benefits of their CCIM association. Thus they can help you identify trade areas rich in the demographics and psychographic groups you seek and can run demographic reports for every site you look at.

An experienced commercial agent will have a familiarity with local lease rates, market conditions, lease structure, commercial zoning, and other relevant local conditions. This can be invaluable and save you much research.

Reasons to go it alone, include keeping yourself free and unfettered to negotiate directly with owners, if they are not represented by an agent, or negotiating directly with an owner's agent, on each property, which could possibly result in less commission being paid on the entire deal, potential (though not necessarily) resulting in a savings to you.

Guerilla site selection: There is a great deal of competition for winning restaurant locations and great rewards for the restaurant owner that can spot a potential location before it becomes obvious to other restaurant owners that it has great restaurant potential and is available.

To find the real gems of potential restaurant locations, it may take diverting your attention away from the "what is" (restaurant-suitable locations currently on the market) and instead focusing on "what could be." I call this strategy "guerilla site location." With this approach you might seek out underserved pockets that you could cobble together into a viable trade area. Or you might focus on identifying neighborhoods that are rapidly gentrifying or improving and work to secure and repurpose an existing non-restaurant building in one of these areas. Or you might seek out a cozy residential-feeling location near a major pocket of employment and open the only independent locally owned restaurant in the area.

Maybe you will repurpose a historical building, a local landmark. The essence of guerilla site selection is seeing potential in neighborhoods and buildings that is not evident to others and seeing and capitalizing on neighborhood change.

THE SINGLE MOST CONSEQUENTIAL DECISION

Finding your ideal site may take abundant time, patience, and diligence. It also requires the ability to confidently say "no," to reject sites that may seem viable but, in your gut, you know are not "it" or that, in your due diligence investigation, are revealed to be unsuitable, or too costly to adapt to your use.

Remember that a bad site is far worse than no site at all. I say this because if you select a bad site your restaurant will struggle with the adverse implications for as long as you are in business. If you select no site, you are in a position to wait until the right one comes up and then to take advantage of it. So don't be in a hurry. Your selection of a home for your restaurant will likely be the single most consequential decision you will make in your process of opening it. Give it the time and attention it merits.

Nine

Will it be profitable? Modeling the financial viability of your potential restaurant

Before investing significant time or money in opening a restaurant, you need to have a clear idea of whether or not it is likely to be profitable. Although in reality it is difficult to predict precisely any new business' exact bottom line, it nonetheless behooves you to model potential income and expenses with as much thoroughness, diligence, and prudence as you possibly can. If you do it well, modeling can reveal both hidden potential as well as hidden flaws and unrealistic assumptions in your restaurant concept. If your modeling indicates profitability, and you proceed, you can continue to use the model, revising it as you obtain new information, to see if the updated analysis still indicates profitability. A well-researched model will provide you with milestones for both income and expenses so that you can track deviations from your model that might reduce or enhance your profitability.

At this point in the process, I will assume that you have selected a potential location for your restaurant and are asking yourself if, based on the characteristics of the potential customers in the trade area surrounding the prospective site, and based on the competitors already in business in the area, there is enough business available, in terms of potential gross sales, to support your restaurant. And, based on the specific cost of the real estate and other expenses, will it be profitable?

PREDICTING GROSS SALES

To be useful, a financial model must accurately project both potential income and expenses. The income projection must be logical and based on real, verifiable data from your trade area.

Projecting income is by nature more difficult than projecting expenses because of the sheer number of variables involved in a customer's decision to select one restaurant over another, or none at all. We will look at two different approaches to projecting your restaurant's potential income, or annual gross sales, each utilizing different sets of assumptions and completely different methodology.

The assumption underlying the first approach is that by opening a restaurant in a given trade area you will not increase the per capita, or total, restaurant spending in that area. Just the opposite. Let's assume something more conservative: a zero-sum scenario wherein any sales you generate will be at the expense of the existing restaurants that draw their customers from the trade area surrounding your proposed restaurant site.

Let us also then assume that, once established, your restaurant will be able to achieve a market share, or percentage of, the existing total similar restaurant sales in its trade area, based on how the existing restaurant's trade areas overlap yours. To envision this, think of a lone restaurant existing in a trade area, capturing 100 percent of the available business, or the entire market share, for that trade area. Suppose you were to open up a very similar restaurant right next door, offering the same fare at the same price. Your restaurant and the existing one would have a virtually the same trade area (100 percent overlap). Therefore, you might expect to eventually split the available business, with each restaurant ending up with a 50 percent market share. But if you opened your restaurant some distance away, so that your trade are overlapped the original restaurant's trade area by only 30 percent, you would then be splitting the business in that 30 percent area in half, thereby reducing the business of the first restaurant by only 15 percent and giving it to yourself.

This may seem to be an overly optimistic assumption, as there is no guarantee that your potential restaurant will be able to effectively compete with established ones and to take significant market share from them. However, this approach, though not exact, is nonetheless useful because it can reveal to you the amount of gross sales potentially up for grabs in your trade area, should you be able to capture a proportional market share that would be sufficient for your restaurant to be profitable. If you find that even with capturing a share of the existing market in proportion to trade area shared with competing restaurants there would still be insufficient gross sales to insure your profitability, then it would probably be best to find another concept that would have fewer competitors or find another trade area. Put another way, this approach can help you identify if there are already too many competing similar-concept restaurants in an area to make your success likely based on the division of existing gross sales in the area.

We will be using this assumption, that similar competing restaurants divide market share proportionally based on overlaps in their trade areas to first determine the total similar restaurant gross sales in the trade area surrounding your prospective site, and then to divide the sales between the existing restaurants and your planned one in order to extrapolate the potential annual gross sales for your restaurant.

For the purposes of identifying existing competing restaurants, "similar-type" would mean meal offered (if you are planning on opening a breakfast and lunch concept restaurant, a dinner-only fine-dining restaurant or a bar offering incidental bar food would not be viewed as a competitor) and service type (a fast food concept would not likely compete with a fast-casual concept restaurant and compete very little with a fine dining one).

To begin the analysis, you will need to determine the annual gross sales for all restaurants whose trade area overlaps the one surrounding your proposed restaurant. You can do this using direct, in-person observation of your existing competitors. You will be observing, recording, and extrapolating the annual gross sales volume from every restaurant that draws customers from your trade area, since you are first trying to determine the total similar-type restaurant sales attributable to your trade area.

First you will need to determine the geographic boundaries of the trade area surrounding your potential site. Your trade area is, by definition, the geographic area where 70 percent of your customers will come from, be they residents or daytime workers. So how do you determine the boundaries of this geographic area from where the vast majority of your customers will come?

Variables that impact the size and shape of a trade area include:

- **Population density** (the greater the density of people, the smaller the size of geographic market area required to provide a sufficient number of customers to sustain your restaurant)
- **Drive times** (the more quickly and easily someone can drive to your restaurant, the further they will be willing to travel to reach it)
- **Price point** (the lower the price point, generally the shorter the distance people will travel; and the higher the price point, the further the distance people will travel to patronize your restaurant – people are willing to drive a greater distance for a rare celebratory dinner as compared to a more casual meal)
- **Geographic barriers** (for instance, a difficult-to-cross freeway, river, or rough area customers may not want to walk through)

Also, the nature of your restaurant concept will determine in part the size of your trade area. Customers may be unwilling to travel more than a short distance for lunch, but will travel longer for dinner, or for a brunch, when there is less time pressure. Customers may be willing to travel a slightly longer distance if there is limited competition for your food type (for instance, if you are the only purveyor in town of a certain ethnic cuisine), or if you develop a particular reputation for excellence.

Identifying the boundaries of your trade area will likely be imprecise, and usually that will be fine. After all, if you err toward too large in determining your trade area boundaries, your trade area will encompass more competitors, diluting the impact of the error. The converse is true as well. If you make the boundaries overly small, you are eliminating from your model both customers and competitors, presumably in equal measure, diminishing the impact of any error.

A trade area always exists surrounding the site, or business, being studied. If people travel equally from all directions, the trade area would resemble a circle with your site in the center. However, if people do not come equally from all directions, the shape of your trade area would change. For instance, if your site was backed up against a long straight river, and there was no bridge for many miles, your trade area might resemble a semi-circle. If you are using drive time to establish a trade area, the area will be pinched out, or extended along more major streets due to the traffic having a higher speed.

For simplicity, you might start by plotting your trade area as a circle on a map, with your site located at the center. You can then consider different radii for the size of the circle. Typical sizes are 0.5 mile and 1 mile. Next, identify existing restaurants whose own trade area might overlap yours. Draw a same-sized circle around each of them so that you can see the extent of the overlap between their presumed trade area and yours.

Direct observation method of calculating a competitor's weekly gross sales: how much money are people currently spending on similar-type restaurants in your potential trade area?

Once you have established the boundaries of your potential trade area, and identified competing restaurants whose trade area overlaps yours, the next step will be to estimate each competitor's gross sales per year.

How do you estimate the annual gross sales of an existing restaurant? Unfortunately, there is generally no easy, publicly available, accurate source for this data, so you will have to estimate it yourself, using direct observation and extrapolation.

The general methodology is this:

1. Select several representative time periods for observation, say, 10 or 15 minutes at the establishment's apparent peak times, slowest times, and several times in between.
2. Sit at a table that allows you to observe either the entire dining room, in the case of a table service restaurant; or the cashier, in the case of a counter-service restaurant.
3. For the duration of each time period, observe and record the number of meals sold, or other items sold, and multiply by the price of the average entrée and drink to determine the approximate dollar volume of sales for the period of time you are observing.
4. Multiply the length of the increment of time you have observed to determine the restaurant's sales volume per hour.
5. Do this during different days of the week and different times of the day so that you have a sales volume per hour for each of these conditions.

Create a spreadsheet with cells for all hours the establishment is open, and designate each hour as having a low, medium, high, or super-high volume, with each categorization defined by a certain hourly dollar volume of business based on your observations.

As an example, a small breakfast and lunch café might have during the weekdays high-volume peaks early in the morning where, based on your observations and notes, you calculate their gross sales as being $400 to $500 per hour, followed by a medium-volume period, for which you calculate their gross sales as $300 to $400 per hour, that transitions into a slow period in mid-morning, for which your observations indicate gross sales are $200 to $300 per hour, and so on.

With your spreadsheet complete, showing an estimated sales volume for each hour, based on several periods of observation, you can now calculate a projected weekly sales volume for the restaurant and multiply to get the annual sales volume. Avoid making your observations on weeks that may be particularly busy or slow based on national holidays or unusual weather.

This may sound like a lot of work, and it can be, but keep in mind that you can, during the course of one week, monitor a number of different restaurants simultaneously, and you can also hire someone to do this work for you or for a nominal amount of money, or you can assemble a team to spread out and monitor several different restaurants at the same times.

Obviously, this method is not highly accurate. There is a lot of rounding, and you are not observing all day, every day, so you may be off on your allocation of slow, medium, busy, and super-busy times. However, when I have used this method on my own restaurants and compared my observations and resulting calculated projected gross with the actual gross sales, I am within 10 percent, close enough for our purposes.

PROPORTIONING COMPETITOR'S GROSS SALES TO YOUR TRADE AREA.

Now you have an informed, observation-based, estimate of the annual gross sales of each restaurant whose trade area overlaps that of your potential restaurant. Next, to get a sense of the total existing restaurant gross sales in your potential trade area, you will need to allocate the gross sales for each competitor based the overlap of their trade area with yours because you care only about the percentage of their sales that come from the trade area surrounding your potential location.

Envision a circle with a one-mile radius with your restaurant site at the center, and another circle, also with a one-mile radius, for a competing restaurant that is just over a mile away. The two circles overlap, but by what percentage? This is important because you will be allocating only the percentage of gross sales from that competitor to the gross sales in your trade area that corresponds to the percentage of overlap of the two circular trade areas.

If you are mathematically inclined, or have a friend who is, you can quickly find a formula online that will allow you to calculate the area of each overlap. If you are less mathematically inclined, I would suggest you do this simple exercise:

1. Cover the circles on your map with a piece of gridded tracing paper.
2. Color the overlapping area one color.
3. Color the non-overlapping area another color.
4. Count the squares (rounding squares that sit on the circumference of any circle up or down, based on whether they are mostly filled in or not).
5. Divide the number of squares in the overlap by the number of squares in the entire circle to determine the percentage of overlap.

After you have determined the area of overlap between each competitor's trade area and yours, you can construct a table showing each competitor's annual gross sales, and their percentage of overlap. By multiplying their estimated annual gross sales by the percentage of overlap, you can determine the amount of gross sales they are drawing from your potential trade area. By totaling all of the various different competitor's gross sales from your trade area, you can estimate the total annual gross restaurant sales currently occurring in your trade area.

EXAMPLE

You determine that for a particular site you are considering, your trade area can be represented by a circle around the site with a one-mile radius and that the trade areas of the nearby existing restaurants – existing restaurants A, B, and C – have similar-size trade areas.

On a map you identify each existing restaurant and, to scale, draw a circle around each, representing a one-mile radius trade area. You note any overlaps in the trade areas and quantify them, either mathematically or using a gridded tracing paper, and convert them to a percentage, as described above. You then multiply the percentage overlap of each trade area by the annual gross sales you have projected for that restaurant based on your observation and extrapolation.

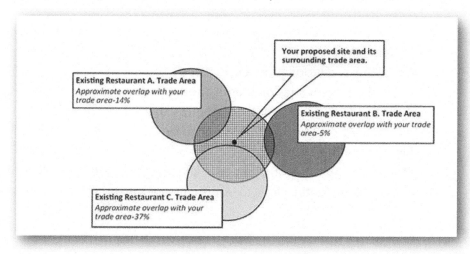

Your proposed site and its surrounding trade area.

Existing Restaurant A. Trade Area
Approximate overlap with your trade area-14%

Existing Restaurant B. Trade Area
Approximate overlap with your trade area-5%

Existing Restaurant C. Trade Area
Approximate overlap with your trade area-37%

You then total all of the gross sales that you have allocated to the trade area surrounding your potential restaurant to determine the total annual gross sales same-type restaurant sales that are already occurring in the trade area.

	Percentage Overlap	Estimated Annual Gross Sales	Gross Sales Attributable to Your Trade Area
Your proposed restaurant			
Existing restaurant A	14%	$2,200,000	$308,000
Existing restaurant B	5%	$1,850,000	$92,500
Existing restaurant C	37%	$3,700,000	$1,369,000
Total Gross Annual Sales Attributable to Trade Area			$1,769,500

Again, the assumption we will use is that your new restaurant will earn some percentage of the dollars-per-week spent on food sales and that, no matter how wonderful and compelling your new restaurant may be, it will not in itself cause people in your trade area to spend more money eating out than they currently do, but rather will cause them, sometime, to eat at your restaurant rather than some other competing restaurant. I believe that this is generally a prudent, conservative, and realistic assumption when applied to any mature market. If you are in an immature market, one that is substantially underserved, where pent-up demand for restaurants in general, or for a particular food or operational type may exist, then this model may be too conservative. We will discuss how to proceed in that case.

CALCULATING THE PERCENTAGE OF EXISTING TRADE AREA SALES YOU WILL LIKELY CAPTURE

Now that you have an idea of the total sales in your trade area, what percentage should you assume you will earn? To start, we will assume that, over time, you will earn a proportional share of the pie, in which case you can divide the total sales for the market area by the total number of competitors, weighing each competitor based on how much of its trade area lies within your trade area.

In our example, we are assuming every trade area is circular, of the same radius, and that different competitors' trade area overlaps yours but not each other's.

	Percentage Overlap	Project Annual Gross Sales	Gross Sales Attributable to Your Trade Area
Your proposed restaurant	100%		
Existing restaurant A	14%	$2,200,000	$308,000
Existing restaurant B	5%	$1,850,000	$92,500
Existing restaurant C	37%	$3,700,000	$1,369,000
Total	156%		$1,769,500

Divide the percentage of your trade are that your restaurant will occupy (100 percent) by the total percentages of it that all existing restaurants combined with yours will occupy (in this example 15 percent). In this case, if you assumed that if you can compete equally with existing competitors who are drawing from the same trade area, you will receive 64.5 percent (100/156 = 64.5) of the available business, or $1,141,327 (64.5 percent of $1,769,500) in gross annual sales.

Again, this approach is admittedly simplistic in that it does not directly account for differences in draw for each restaurant based on different levels of appeal; it assumes they all compete equally. Nonetheless, this can give you a rough but still very valuable idea of the amount of restaurant gross sales that a given trade area is currently generating. As well, knowing your competitor's gross sales can be invaluable later on in setting your own sales benchmarks.

You may be attempted to made adjustments based on negative attributes of some of your competitors (small dining room, poor food quality, etc.) and the positive attributes you hope to have, but I would be very careful with this. Your competitors have established clientele, and can also modify and improve their operation in response to yours, fighting to keep their market share.

It may be that in your prospective trade area there is unmet, or pent-up, demand, a gap between the number of capacity of the existing restaurants and the potential demand from the residents or workers in your trade area. This is an ideal situation, allowing you to attract available customers without having to wrest them away from existing competitors. What is the process then for determining if there is unmet demand for your potential restaurant in a given trade area and if there is, quantifying it?

GAP ANALYSIS

Market gap analysis is the process of using demographic data to project the demand for a given category of retail, such as restaurants, in a given location, based on the consumption habits of the residents or daytime workers in the trade area as indicated by their demographic characteristics. A market gap analysis weighs the projected demand within a given geographically defined area with the supply of the same category of item in the same area, as indicated by existing competitors, and identifies a gap if the projected demand exceeds the supply. For instance, an analysis of the demographics of a certain trade area might indicate that based on the size and demographic makeup of the population of the trade area, average spending on fine dining might be projected to be $10 million per year. That figure would then be weighed against the estimated gross annual sales of restaurants in, or drawing from, the same trade area. If the combined sales of those restaurants equaled $8 million, it could be assumed that the gap, the amount of unmet need, would be the difference between these numbers, $2 million per year.

How do you actually go about completing a gap analysis? There are a number of good suppliers of demographic information and mapping and analysis tools that allow one to do this sort of analysis (see list at end of this chapter). However, the difficulty is that their business model is to charge annual subscriptions, usually between $1,000 and $2,000 per year, rather than to charge on an individual report basis. A few suppliers do allow for monthly subscriptions which are priced in the range of $500 per month. If you are doing in-depth analysis and evaluation of many prospective sites, despite the high cost, this may be money well spent. An alternative is to enlist the aid of an experienced commercial real estate broker who specializes in retail sales and leases. Most retail brokers have access to one of the major proprietary demographic and psychographic mapping and analysis providers and will be willing to generate reports on each location that they show you including a market gap.

Using either approach, direct observation and harvesting of data from the existing competitors in your trade area or a market gap analysis based on the demographics and gross sales of existing competitors, or a combination of both approaches, you can begin to estimate a conservative gross annual sales potential for your restaurant. If there are substantial disparities in the physical size of any of the competing restaurants and yours, you may need to adjust the data accordingly.

PROJECTING YOUR EXPENSES

Labor: You can projected your labor costs either directly, assuming certain levels of staffing throughout the day and applying local market labor rates, or you can apply a ratio to your projected gross sales.

To directly estimate labor costs, create a spreadsheet with your planned hours of operation which indicates staffing levels for each hour (e.g., 10:00 a.m. to 11:00 a.m., two line cooks, one prep cook, one cashier, one food runner/busser, one dishwasher), enter an hourly compensation per position, and calculate a labor cost for each hour of operation and for pre-opening and for closing times. Add up the direct costs of labor and then increase by the amount of payroll taxes and benefits (which will vary by state). This will give you an approximate absolute cost of labor, if your staffing levels are accurate.

For the majority of restaurants, cost of labor varies between 28 percent and 33 percent of the gross sales of the establishment. Calculate your labor using this range as well to make sure that the number you come up with using the prior method is in the ballpark of this industry range.

FOOD COSTS

Your cost of food will likely be between 25 and 35 percent of your gross sales. This can vary substantially with the type of concept and food offered. Foods such as pizza have a much lower cost of ingredients relative to price, and fine-dining concept restaurants generally having a much higher ratio of food cost to gross sales. For the purposes of this initial "cocktail napkin" examination of profitability, unless your concept entails a cost of food that would push you to either extreme of the continuum, you will likely be safe with 33 percent of your gross sales.

COST OF OCCUPANCY

You can directly and accurately calculate your cost of occupancy using the actual rent or mortgage payment required for the location you are considering. Add to the rent any additional building expenses that you will be responsible for: property taxes, property hazard insurance, common area maintenance, building maintenance, etc. Add to that the cost of your utilities.

EQUIPMENT MAINTENANCE, REPAIR, AND REPLACEMENT

How much you will spend annually on equipment repairs largely depends on the age and condition of the equipment, but during the course of any year, on average, you will likely have repairs and routine maintenance, and replacement. You can approximate an average amount by amortizing the value of the equipment over a relatively short period, again depending on the age and condition.

You should include both an annual figure for equipment replacement based on an amortization of a reasonable remaining life of the equipment and an annual figure for maintenance and repair of the equipment. For new equipment the life might be relatively long, perhaps 10 or 15 years, depending on the type of equipment. As well, annual repairs will likely be much less than with used equipment.

Used equipment will likely have a much shorter life and its value should be amortized over three to five years. As well, you will need to budget more for repairs.

Example: You open with $50,000 of used refrigeration and other kitchen equipment. The condition of the equipment is good and will have a service life of five years, so you amortize the $50,000 over five years, allocating $10,000 per year for equipment replacement. Additionally, based on consultation with a refrigeration equipment service company, you allocate $1,500 per year for repairs.

Clearly there are a number of pieces of equipment that seldom break down and don't require replacement frequently, such as prep tables, exhaust hood, counters, etc. and, to make a reasonable accounting of your cost of equipment replacement and repair, you will likely not need to include these items.

TRANSACTION FEES

You will need to calculate the annual merchant fees for the percentage of gross sales handled through credit and debit cards. Consult with a merchant services provider for a reasonable estimate of both.

ADVERTISING

Include an annual budget for advertising. Even if eventually you find no need for paid advertising, it will likely be necessary to get established. One to 3 percent of gross sales is not unreasonable.

OTHER MONTHLY SERVICES

Include any reoccurring expenses such as: alarm monitoring, monthly POS system licensing, pest control, linen and cloth laundering, etc.

DETERMINING PROFIT OR LOSS

Total all of your annual expenses and subtract them from the annual gross sales number you estimated through either the direct competitor observation method or from a gap analysis done using proprietary demographic information. The resulting number is your profit or loss. If the number is negative, it may be that the trade area you are considering does not have the potential to generate a volume of gross sales sufficient for an additional restaurant in the area, and of the type you are planning, to be profitable.

On the other hand, you may be able to wrest business from your existing competitors in the area, but this is a risky assumption. You may introduce a new concept, offer higher-quality food, service, or atmosphere, but the existing competitors will likely modify their performance, and up their game, to avoid a hemorrhage of business.

It may be that the existing competitors are offering a not-easily modified concept, like fast food, and you will be offering, something different, like fast casual. In that case, a gap analysis based on the demographics and psychographic characteristics of the residents and workers in the trade area is likely to provide a better sense of the potential demand for your potential restaurant than the direct observation method.

Demographic and site analysis resources:
sitesusa.com
segmentationsolutions.nielsen.com
idealspot.com

Ten

Negotiating the lease for your restaurant

L ikely your first restaurant will be in a leased location, which will help you to conserve your capital and keep your options open should the location turn out to be less than ideal for your concept. In any market there will generally be many more properties available for lease than for purchase. This is true because investors generally hold on to buildings that are ideally situated for restaurants and because many spaces available for lease will be a portion of a larger, multi-tenant retail center, which would not be feasible to purchase.

THE PROCESS

You may work with a commercial real estate agent who will be representing your interests, or you may negotiate directly with the landlord's leasing agent, or you may negotiate directly with a landlord who is not being represented by a leasing agent. In either case, your initial goal should be the acquisition of market-specific knowledge. Gather as much information as possible about as many spaces as possible with the goal of understanding the market for restaurant space in your area.

Put as much of the data you gather as you can into a spreadsheet so that you can make adjustments for the differing sizes, conditions, and costs associated with each space. Your goal in creating this spreadsheet is to reduce the competing properties to some common denominator of pricing and to highlight major differences between each.

When you narrow your list down to one space and decide to make an offer on it, the negotiating vehicle will be a letter of intent (LOI). If there is a leasing agent involved in the transaction usually they will draft the LOI based on information that you give them covering all of the deal points: the lease rate, the lease term, the division of expenses, etc. The LOI is almost always non-binding and is simply an organized, written vehicle for negotiations. If the LOI is ultimately accepted by both parties, it becomes the basis for the lease document, which is legally binding on all parties.

LEASE STRUCTURE

Before beginning to shop around and compare available lease spaces, it is important to understand the varying types of lease structures and who pays for what in each structure. We can think of any lease, and the division of which costs the tenant pays for and which the landlord pays for, as existing at some point on a continuum. On one end of the continuum would be leases where essentially all expenses associated with the property – property taxes, hazard insurance, and maintenance – are paid by the tenant in addition to the rent. This may be referred to as a net lease, or commonly as a triple net lease (often abbreviated as NNN) and is very typical for many freestanding buildings, particularly in high-demand areas.

On the other end of the continuum would be a gross, or full-service, lease. In a purely gross lease the tenant pays one fixed amount for rent and the landlord pays all of the costs associated with property including property taxes, building hazard insurance, and building maintenance.

In actuality, very few leases are purely net or gross leases but a hybrid of the two. For instance, perhaps a tenant might pay for interior maintenance and minor exterior maintenance, and the landlord might cover maintenance to major components such as the roof and basic building structure. Perhaps the tenant might pay for utilities that they use and the landlord pays for property taxes. In many cases the structure of the lease is subject to negotiation.

It is essential to understand the proposed lease structure offered for each space under consideration so that you can make an apples-to-apples cost comparison. For instance, if you are comparing one space where the landlord is offering a lease that includes property taxes and building insurance with a space that is offered on an NNN basis, you will need to be able to quantify the monthly or annual cost of those expenses in order to accurately compare the costs to occupy each space.

In the case of a lease for a space in a multi-tenant retail center, it is typical for the cost of common area maintenance, the parking lot and similar shared space, to be passed through to the tenant on a pro-rata basis. The total annual cost of these items for the entire shopping center are divided by the square footage of the entire property to determine an amount per square foot leased that will be "passed through" annually to each tenant.

Assuming that the net cost to you, the tenant, is the same, which sort of lease structure, is best for you as a restaurant tenant? It depends. There may be greater security and predictability of future expenses for you if the landlord is responsible for expenses that could increase annually such as property taxes. As well, it may not make sense for you as a tenant to be solely responsible for the cost of replacing major components, such as heating and air conditioning units, whose life may exceed the duration of your lease. On the other hand, if a risk such as a sudden increase in property taxes is shouldered exclusively by the landlord, he or she will likely ask some additional rent to compensate for the additional risk.

Typically rent is calculated based on a price per square foot. However, a lease may also be negotiated where all or some portion of the lease amount will be determined by the gross sales of the business. This is called a percentage lease. In a percentage lease there may be a floor, the minimum amount that a tenant pays irrespective of sales, and a ceiling, a maximum amount that the tenant would pay no matter how high their sales. Generally after a certain monthly sales threshold is reached, the tenant pays a negotiated percentage of sales above that point.

Initially the idea of paying a percentage of your sales to your landlord may seem like anathema. However, it can have some appealing advantages as compared to a fixed rate lease. In many ways a lease rate that varies every month depending on the sales of your restaurant can serve to align your interests as the restaurant owner with those of the landlord. For instance, under a standard lease where the monthly rent is determined solely by the rent rate per square foot and the number of square feet your restaurant occupies, if midway through a multi-year lease you were to ask the landlord to make a major investment in the leased space, such as expanding the kitchen, the landlord would have little incentive to do so. The rent has long ago been negotiated and would not increase as a result of the landlord's new investment. However, under a lease where part or all of the lease rate is determined by your monthly gross sales, if the landlord's improvements and new investment in the space could be convincingly demonstrated to cause a substantial increase in the tenant's gross sales, and in turn the percentage rent paid to the landlord, the landlord might consider the new investment a profitable business decision with a potentially high return on investment.

For a restaurant owner expenses that are variable relative to their sales volume, such as the cost of food, or labor, are less risky than those that are constant irrespective of ups and downs in monthly sales such as a fixed monthly rental amount. Having a rental agreement that converts your monthly rent to a variable, rather than a fixed, expense, may significantly reduce your risk associated with periods of slow sales or when the restaurant is still new and trying to get established. By reducing your rent during slow times at the cost of increasing it during very busy times you may be increasing both your restaurants stability and sustainability.

Other potentially negotiable lease considerations include:

Lease Rate: The lease rate, the amount that you will pay per square foot per month or year, is negotiated with the building owner and then stipulated by the lease. Additionally, any scheduled increases in that rate, which can either be by a fixed amount per year or by a percentage increase every year, are spelled out in the lease.

What is a fair lease rate? Just like any other commodity, lease rates are determined by supply and demand. It is worth familiarizing yourself with the asking rates on as many properties as possible in the geographic areas in which you are looking, putting them all in a spreadsheet, and adjusting by any additional expenses you would be responsible for (property taxes, etc.) so that you have an equal basis for comparison.

Some commercial real estate brokers will be highly informed and experienced in a given market and will work with their landlords to price lease properties at very near the current market value. However, commercial real estate brokers are generally not restaurant owners and may miss key differences that serve to give one property substantially more profit potential for a restaurant owner than another. Ultimately it is up to you to derive your own sense of both a fair lease rate as determined by the market and a lease rate that is tenable for you, based on the exact economics of your restaurant and your budget for rent.

Duration: One of the biggest, most serious considerations of any lease is the term. If you are leasing space for a new restaurant, as the owner will likely be asked to personally guarantee the lease. This means that if the restaurant fails you will still financially responsible for the lease payment until another tenant occupies the space. For a first restaurant in particular, I suggest extreme prudence when considering committing to a long-term lease.

A short-term lease would seem to reduce your risk as the restaurant owner, allowing for the potential that your new restaurant won't be profitable or that another location ends up being much better suited for your concept. However, a short-term lease presents its own risk. At the expiration of the lease, particularly if the restaurant is obviously successful, the landlord is free to increase the rent dramatically. Or, worse yet, another restaurant owner might approached the building owner, perhaps offering a higher rent, and make a deal to lease the space at the expiration of your lease.

So if both long- and short-term leases are risky, what is the ideal lease term for the owner of a new restaurant? From nearly 30 years of experience negotiating commercial leases professionally, I have two strategies for risk mitigation when negotiating a lease for an untested restaurant. My approach is to negotiate an initial short-lease term but to also negotiate that the lease includes several options for longer extensions of it.

For instance, you might negotiate an initial lease term of one year and three options to extend the lease for periods of five years each. The initial term of one year is important as many new restaurants decide to close in their first year. Using this lease structure, at the end of the first year of operations, you can take a serious look at your restaurant's profitability and decide whether to close, move to a different location, or exercise the lease option and commit for five more years. At the end of the six and 11th year you would have the same options; to terminate the lease without penalty or to exercise another of the five-year options. Under this arrangement the original one year lease could result in a 16-year lease without the possibility of an increase in rent beyond what was originally agreed to for each option period during the original lease negotiations. This lease structure will give you a reasonably low-cost out, should you decide to close at the location after a year, or after each five-year increment, but will also protect you from unforeseen rent increases in the event that your restaurant is a runaway success.

Another approach, in the event that the landlord is very resistant to a one-year or similar short-term lease, would be to negotiate a longer term lease with an early termination clause which, in exchange for reimbursing the landlord for any unamortized expenses associated with initiation of the lease, would allow you to cancel the lease early with no further liability.

Typically landlords will have certain up-front costs as a result of entering into a lease agreement. These can be substantial and might include the commission paid to the leasing agent (usually some percentage of the total amount of the entire lease) and the costs of any improvements to the space that the landlord agrees to make. In negotiating a lease the landlord will typically use a base lease rate, an amount that that they will accept for the lease of the space itself, and then add to that the monthly amount required to amortize the amount of their front-end expenditure over the entire term of the lease, at some interest rate. For example, if a landlord has $50,000 in front-end costs in order to complete a 10-year lease agreement, and decides that their opportunity cost, the rate of return they could earn in other available investments, is 6 percent per year, they would add $551.10 to the monthly rent to recover, or amortize, the $50,000 and 6 percent interest over the term of the 10-year lease.

In the event of an early termination of a lease, say if the business fails, the landlord risks not being able to recover the unamortized portion of these front-end expenses. This is the primary reason that landlords are concerned with a potential tenant's credit and ask for personal guarantees.

The key to negotiating a provision in a lease that will allow you to terminate the lease without ongoing liability is for the tenant to agree to make the landlord whole by reimbursing them for the unamortized portion of any front-end expenses that they incurred in making the lease. When I have represented tenants in commercial lease negotiations and proposed that the tenant have an option to cancel the lease before its term by paying the landlord's unamortized costs associated with initiating the lease, I have nearly always had the proposal accepted by the landlord. For the tenant the cost associated with canceling the lease now diminishes every month and can be calculated to the penny so as to better inform decision-making.

Exclusive use: If you are negotiating a lease in a retail center, a competitor moving into the same center could be extremely damaging to your business. Depending on the size of the retail center, it may be worth negotiating a provision that excludes the landlord in that center from leasing to any other restaurants, or, if that is not reasonable, from leasing to restaurants with the same or similar concept and offerings as yours. Do not assume that the tenants in place when you move in will always remain there. Imagine them moving out and being replaced by restaurants that directly compete with you. If that is not an appealing prospect, consider negotiating an exclusive-use provision.

In the case where parking is not exclusive to your premises and shared, such as in a retail center, you must evaluate how the customers of other businesses use the shared parking spaces. Gyms have peak times early in the morning and early in the evening, which might monopolize parking spaces during your dinner service. Theatres can be parking space hogs, particularly during evenings and weekends. It is worthwhile to observe the parking lots for spaces you are considering leasing during numerous times of day to see what the actual availability of spaces will be for your customers based on the ebb and flow of parking spaces used by customers of surrounding businesses.

Tenant improvements: As part of a negotiated lease the landlord may agree to make certain improvements to the property, like adding a commercial kitchen or making the minimum improvements required to permit the legal use of the property as a restaurant. In considering whether to take the risk of investing money in improvements, the landlord first will consider your financial strength as a tenant, seeking assurance that you can be depended on you to make the lease payment through the duration of the lease, allowing the landlord to recoup their investment in the space. This suggests a strategy for the tenant. If you cannot demonstrate financial strength or are trying to negotiate a short-term lease, focus on spaces that require little of no modification. By reducing the landlord's risk, you may open more doors for yourself.

CAN YOU AFFORD IT?

Perhaps the single more important question to ask with any lease space is whether your new restaurant can afford it. Specifically, is the amount of the rent, and the combined amount of the rent plus other costs associated with your occupancy of the space, within the range budgeted for it as a percentage of your gross sales?

It's important to distinguish between rent and cost of occupancy, as there are different allowable ratios between each and your gross sales. Your rent is strictly what you pay for use of the space while cost of occupancy is that number plus any other property costs you may be responsible for, such as property taxes, property insurance, utilities, etc.

A general restaurant industry rule of thumb is that your rent should not exceed 5 to 8 percent of your gross sales. If it does creep up even a few points above this amount, you will likely be shaving those points from your bottom line net profit. Worse yet, in slow periods and during your startup period, those points may be coming out of your pocket.

Another rule of thumb is that your total cost of occupancy should not exceed 8 to 10 percent of your gross sales. It can be tempting to accept a lease with a cost higher than the above ratios, with the justification that your business will grow sufficiently to offset the additional cost. This thinking can be a fallacy, as the superior location or other desirability of the space has already been taken into account in your gross sales projections for that location. There are some restaurants that have business models that make either the cost of food to gross sales or the cost of labor to gross sales substantially below normal (for instance, with a high-end bar), which allows them to pay a higher percentage of their gross sales as rent in order to secure an ideal location. But for a first restaurant, it is best to keep both the rent and the cost of occupancy within industry-accepted ratios.

Eleven

Negotiating a real estate purchase for your restaurant

WHY OWN?

There are a plethora of advantages to owning the building that will house your restaurant.

Leasing a building may make you vulnerable to rent increases. The combination of a very successful restaurant combined with the high cost to your restaurant of relocating creates a situation where the landlord may have the upper hand and may be able to command ever-increasing rent rates, which over time may erode your restaurant's bottom line profitability.

Unlike with a leased premises, your rent will never increase. With a standard mortgage the principal and interest portion of your mortgage payment will remain a constant until you pay off the mortgage and then have no payment. As your restaurant sales rise, a constant mortgage payment will consume a smaller and smaller percentage of your gross sales.

Owning your own building also gives you a greater degree of flexibility in the future, if and when you ever sell your restaurant. The value of your restaurant, for the purposes of a sale, is dependent upon your bottom-line profits, and these profits are negatively impacted by increasing rent. In other words, the higher the rent, the lower the net profits, the lower the value of the business. In comparison, if you own the building and keep it but someday sell the business, you can negotiate the lease rate as part of the sale negotiations. A lower-than-market lease would likely enhance the sales price of your restaurant. As well, keeping the building and eventually selling your business may make for an excellent retirement plan.

Remodeling increases property value. If you own the real estate, the many thousands, or hundreds of thousands, of dollars you spend remodeling to improving the property will accrue to your benefit, adding value to the property, rather than accruing to your landlord's benefit.

As owner of the building, you also will have the flexibility to modify the property as your restaurant grows and changes, a freedom you may not have with a leased property.

You could save money on your taxes. If you hold the building in an entity apart from the entity owning the restaurant as an investment property and lease it to your restaurant enterprise, you may enjoy certain tax advantages. The annual depreciation, or cost recovery, as it is technically called, that you are allowed for the purposes of federal taxation will offset income earned from the property. This can be a significant tax savings.

VALUING THE PROPERTY

After determining the suitability of a given property for your restaurant based on an analysis of its surrounding trade area and other characteristics of the building and its entitlements, you will want to examine the building's value based both on its market value and then on its value to you. Typically, though not always, there will be an appraisal done as part of the building purchase. If there is not an appraisal, there should be some body of work done by the real estate agent listing the property to determine its value. This is usually called a competitive market analysis

(CMA). Whether examining the comparable sales used in an appraisal or the comparable sales the listing agent used in their CMA, it is important that you do your own research by verifying the similarity and applicability of the comparable sales used.

When purchasing real estate for your restaurant, you have additional concerns beyond those of a restaurant owner. You also will have those of any real estate investor, including: Is the price fair? Is the property in an area that will likely appreciate more, or less, than other areas in the same market? If you sell the building, will you be able to recoup the money you spend to improve the property?

Not overpaying for the property is crucial. As the real estate bromide goes, you make your money when you buy, not when you sell. The idea here being that you can always say "no" when you are buying but when you are selling. External circumstances may force you to sell, and you will have much less control over the market conditions at that time.

Any property may have many different values. For instance, the value at which a property is assessed for purposes of taxation, its replacement value, its market value, and its value to you as an investor might each be substantially different from the other. The two values that are most relevant for the purposes of purchasing a building to house your restaurant are the market value and the investor value.

MARKET VALUE
Market value is the value of the property based upon comparisons to other similar nearby properties that have sold. Investor value is the value of the property to a given investor, in this case you, for your particular purpose of opening a new restaurant.

The market value of the property you are considering, the subject property, can be determined by comparing it to properties that have sold. These are called comparable properties. You will give most importance, or weight, to those properties that are nearest to the location the subject property, most similar in terms of age, size, configuration, and zoning, and have sold most recently.

There are a number of different techniques for comparing sold, or comparable, properties to your subject property. The most straightforward, and common, is cost per square foot. What dollar range per square foot have similar properties sold for and how does that compare to the price of the property you are considering? You may need to make adjustments to the comparable properties for differing land sizes, building conditions, etc.

ADJUSTMENTS TO COMPARABLE SALES

Commercial real estate agents typically have little or no restaurant experience and, in my experience, often lack an understanding of restaurant economics that would allow them to accurately compare the ability of one property versus another to produce income from a restaurant. In evaluating the sold comparables from either the appraisal or the agent's CMA, consider:

The trade area surrounding the comparable sale: If the income demographics of the trade area surrounding a comparable sale are significantly different than those surrounding the subject property, this will impact value. For instance, a much higher average household income in a trade area surrounding a site would indicate the potential for higher restaurant profitability, and would require some adjustment when comparing it to a property with a surrounding trade area of much lower income. This adjustment is crucial from the restaurant owner's perspective but is often lacking from restaurant site appraisals.

Traffic: All other things being equal, a restaurant would likely be more profitable on a highly trafficked street. If there is a large difference in traffic volume on streets between a comparable sale site and the site you are considering, there should be some adjustment in value to compensate.

Obsolescence: As both consumer preferences and neighborhood populations change, certain concepts and their resulting restaurant configurations become obsolete. This will vary from market to market. In my market, for instance, former walk-up fast food locations, particularly those lacking both a dining room and a drive-through, are in very low demand, as to adapt them for use as even a small café would require the addition of a dining room and any major modification to a commercial building's footprint can necessitate bringing the entire building into compliance with current building codes, which can be very costly. Nonetheless, I have looked at several of these purely walk-up locations, looked at the CMA done to determine price, and noted that the sold comparables consisted of very usable restaurant locations with dining rooms. Be sure the comparables used are apples-to-apples in regard to largely out-of-date and obsolete facilities.

If a sold comparable property has aspects to it that are substantially better, or worse, you will need to adjust its value accordingly. For instance, if one sold property had 10,000 square feet more land area than your subject property, and you are able to determine that similar land is selling for $20 per square foot, so the additional 10,000 square feet of land probably added $20,000 to the sale price, you would then reduce the sale price by that amount, to make the property most similar to your property. The same principle applies if the comparable property is interior to your property in some quantifiable way. In that case you would add, rather than subtract, some increment of value.

INVESTOR VALUE
A restaurant may be a great deal as indicated by market value, and still be a bad deal for you. If the investor value, the value to you based on your

unique use, is lower than the market value, then likely the location is not for you.

Refer to the profit and loss projections you have already completed. How does the cost of occupancy for the building you are considering (the mortgage payment and all other costs associated with occupying the premises) compare with your budgeted cost of occupancy? If your cost of occupancy is above the amount indicated in your profit and loss projections, which is based on your projected gross annual sales, then the value of the building to you may be lower than the market value of the building. This is an indication that the building is not ideal for your concept, at least at its market value.

CONDUCTING RESTAURANT SITE DUE DILIGENCE

The phrase "due diligence" describes the investigation phase in any commercial real estate purchase. Some due diligence may take place before you make an offer, but the majority of your investigations will likely take place after you have negotiated a purchase, during a contingency period. A partial list of due diligence specific to purchasing real estate for use as a restaurant:

1. **Entitlements:** Is there a legal entitlement to use the property for your intended use? Generally this means, does the existing zoning allow for a restaurant of the size, and with the features you have in mind? If you intend to have a drive-through window, does the existing zoning allow for that?
2. **Parking:** Often, for your restaurant to be approved, a minimum number of parking spaces relative to the size of the building will be required. Does the building and property configuration offer at least the required amount of parking? Regulations aside, is there sufficient parking either onsite or close by, to satisfy the demands of your intended volume of customers?
3. **Utilities:** Does the building have adequate electrical capacity for the equipment you have in mind? If you will be using equipment

that requires three-phase electrical power, is it available at the site? Are the existing gas lines and meter of sufficient size to deliver the volume of natural gas your equipment will require?

4. **Signage:** The signage allowed on a property, like the use of the property, is generally limited by applicable zoning and local ordinance. What sort of signage is allowed (Freestanding, monument, flush-mounted)? What is the total area of signage allowed? Will this be sufficient for your use as a restaurant? Are there any existing signs that may be "grandfathered in," that is, allowed to remain because they predate more restrictive zoning?

5. **Building condition and adequacy:** Depending on the age of the building you may wish to hire a professional building inspector to ascertain the structural integrity of the building and the functionality of the heating, ventilation, air conditioning (HVAC), and electrical systems.

6. **Equipment condition:** If restaurant equipment is included in the purchase, you will want to verify that it works and is adequate for your needs. A refrigeration technician can evaluate the condition and likely remaining life of any walk-in coolers or freezers.

7. **Environmental issues:** If the building had a prior non-restaurant use, like a dry cleaner or manufacturing facility, you will want to be particularly cautious about any existing contamination. In this case you would likely want to hire an environmental engineer to inspect the property.

Owning the building for your restaurant can give you great flexibility and potentially make great long-term financial sense. On the other hand, it puts much more on your plate than would be the case if you were leasing, and purely focused on developing your concept in a leased facility. The best alternative for you will depend on a combination of your finances and what properties are available on the market for lease and for sale.

Twelve

Making it yours: remodeling, equipping, furnishing, and preparing to open

At this point we will assume you have completed the purchase or lease of the building or space that your new restaurant will occupy. This chapter covers the period of time from that point until just before your opening, when you will be completing the design, permitting, and construction required for any renovation and remodeling. As well, you will be purchasing your kitchen equipment and furnishings, and selecting vendors for ancillary systems such as merchant services, security, pest control, etc. You also will be deciding on your hours of operation. And you will be making all of these decisions while feeling some degree of pressure to get the business open and producing income as soon as possible.

SELECTING PROFESSIONALS

If substantial remodeling of your building is required, the production of building plans by an architect will likely be required, as will review and approval of those plans by the relevant governmental agencies. In selecting an architect, find one with significant same-scale restaurant design experience and ask to see their portfolio of similar projects. As well, contact some of their past clients to make sure that their experiences were satisfactory. Also, in your first contact with an architect you are considering using, ask about the time they require to complete the work. I have had the design and drawing production for fairly small-scale and straight-forward restaurant remodels take as little as a week and as long as two months, depending on the architect involved. The architect's fee can be eclipsed by the cost to you of a two-month delay. Also, ask your architect how long the governmental plan review and permitting process is typically taking in your area so that you can incorporate that into your timeline accurately.

Similarly, in deciding on a contractor, find one who has prior experience remodeling commercial kitchens. Do as much online research as possible on each prospective contractor. Contact your state building contractor licensing authority and see if any complaints have been filed against that contractor, and contact prior clients of the contractor. Most architects and contractors are honest and reliable, but there are those in circulation who are highly unreliable and have a long trail of unmet deadlines, unfinished projects, and litigation against them. Doing a moderate amount of research before hiring any building professionals can save you months of aggravation and a greatly delayed opening.

The specific requirements concerning your restaurant design, work permitting, construction, and approval process will vary substantially from municipality to municipality so be clear on what is required for your location.

In addition to any remodeling or repurposing the building or space, you will need to make a plethora of decisions concerning equipment and ancillary systems.

EQUIPMENT

For almost any style of restaurant, equipment will be both a major consideration and a major expense. The first rule is to purchase only equipment that is NSF-rated, or approved for use in a restaurant, and bears the NSF designation. Let's look at some options for equipment acquisition:

New Equipment: Purchasing new equipment gives you the greatest degree of reliability. If much of your kitchen will be visible to customers, new equipment can give you a more desirable, and uniform look. As well, new equipment may be more technologically advanced, making it more energy-efficient and perhaps having features that you won't find in used equipment.

The downside of new equipment is the cost, and the initial depreciation of its value that you will experience. Much like purchasing a new car, most restaurant equipment loses value substantially, up to 50 percent, upon first installation and use. The depreciation can be an important factor, particularly if you are not absolutely sure that the equipment you purchase is exactly ideal for the task at hand, and you may want to soon replace it.

If you decide to purchase new equipment, you can either purchase it from a local restaurant equipment supplier or online. In either case, begin by researching the piece of equipment online in order to determine a competitive price for it, to read any online reviews, and to familiarize yourself with its technical data (e.g., voltage, amperage, BTU, footprint size, etc.). This information will come in handy when you visit a brick-and-mortar showroom.

The advantages of purchasing locally may include: getting to inspect and handle the equipment prior to committing to purchase it, the avoidance of shipping charges, and a much better ability to return the item if it proves unsatisfactory.

There are several very large, well-respected online restaurant equipment sites. The advantages of purchasing new equipment online can include: greater selection, lower price, avoidance of local sales tax, and less time spent on the entire process of making the purchase.

Used Equipment: In the three restaurants I have opened, approximately 90 percent of my equipment has been purchased used. I have done this primarily because of price. On average, for the used equipment I have acquired, I have paid between 20 and 50 percent of the price of comparable new equipment. This has been helpful in those instances where we went down a wrong path and purchased equipment that was ultimately not a good fit for us or when we outgrew a piece of equipment. Having purchased the equipment used, I was able to sell it for about what I had paid for it.

The obvious downsides of purchasing used equipment can be a lack of reliability and a compromised appearance. The fewer the number of electronic and moving mechanical components, the less reliability is of concern. For instance, a used gas range, oven, char grill, or griddle, due to its simplicity, will likely provide only a slight reduction in reliability, or service life, due to being used. On the other hand, a complex piece of refrigeration equipment, say, a blast chiller with a mother board and printer, is more likely to suffer diminished reliability and a reduced service life due to being used.

There are two main ways to go about purchasing used equipment:

1. **Purchasing from a known equipment rebuilder:** There are companies that purchase used equipment, inspect it, repair it as necessary, and resell it. The advantage of purchasing equipment from a company that does this is that the equipment can be demonstrated to be correctly functioning before you pick it up (particularly important for refrigeration equipment), it will be clean, it will come with some level of warranty and, if there is a problem, the seller can be located and has a vested interest in keeping you happy. Also, most rebuilders provide free delivery and installation, a big plus for large pieces of equipment. When purchasing from a restaurant equipment rebuilder, expect to pay 50 to 60 percent of the original

new value of the piece of equipment, depending on its age and condition.

2. **Purchasing from an individual:** A great deal of restaurant equipment trades hands every day from individuals whose restaurants have outgrown equipment or have closed. There are ads every day in Craigslist and similar classifieds for used restaurant equipment, much of it at attractive prices.

   There are a number of challenges to purchasing used restaurant equipment from individuals. The first is that if they closed a restaurant, they usually wish to sell all of the equipment as one lot, for one price. In most cases, if they are trying to sell to another, or a prospective, restaurant owner, rather than to a broker or rebuilder, the "all as one lot" is only attractive to the buyer if they are opening a restaurant of exactly the same type, and size, as the one for which the equipment is being liquidated, which is highly unlikely. I have often run into this dilemma, a former restaurant owner wishing to sell all of their equipment as "one lot", when I have no use for the majority of it. Usually I try to form a connection with the seller, give them my contact information, and let them know that I only have use for a few of the pieces that they are selling. I then contact them from time to time. In most cases they eventually realize that to sell everything in one lot the only prospective buyer is a rebuilder, who would pay perhaps 20 percent of the new value of the equipment, and therefore they are better off selling me the few pieces I am interested in at perhaps 50 percent of the new value, and then selling only the unsold pieces to the rebuilder.

   Another difficulty with purchasing from an individual is that they frequently don't realize the real-world market value of their used equipment and often over-estimate the demand and value substantially. In these cases I make an offer and share photos and prices of competing available new and used equipment, and explain my logic as to the value. I always keep the discussion cordial and leave my contact information. Many of my purchases happen a month or so after I initially viewed the equipment.

Particular care must be taken when purchasing refrigeration equipment as the condition and functionality are not evident by casual inspection. My firm rule is never to purchase refrigeration equipment directly from an individual without that equipment being plugged in, operating, and confirmed to maintain correct temperature. When calling about a piece of refrigeration equipment, always ask if the owner would plug it in an hour or so before you arrive to inspect it. When you show up to view it, bring a refrigerator thermometer so you can verify that the unit is correctly holding temperature.

With purchasing a used ice makers from an individual, make sure that it is plugged in and producing ice before you purchase it.

When purchasing ranges, deep fryers, and similar, if they are dirty, take into account the amount it will cost to thoroughly clean the equipment because it may be considerable. A rebuilder I know calculates that for a very dirty range it may take one of his experienced employees eight hours to thoroughly clean it.

On several occasions I have purchased the contents of entire closed restaurants. In these cases I have created a spreadsheet with every item in the restaurant, graded each piece as to condition and age, and then discounted each from its original new price. This creates a transparency that allows the seller to understand my thinking and see that the final amount I am offering is not arbitrary or "pulled from thin air," but is in fact well-researched and thoroughly considered.

A not-so-obvious advantage of purchasing equipment directly from the owners of failed restaurants is what you can learn in the process. Over the years I've engaged in lengthy conversations with probably 25 or 30 owners of closed restaurants, and these experiences have given me a much greater insight into how and why restaurants fail. I believe any owner of independent restaurants should be a serious student of how and why restaurants fail and take advantage of every opportunity to learn more about it.

Furnishings: Just as is the case with equipment, you can purchase furnishings, particularly tables and chairs, either new or used, and either from a brick and mortar store or online. I have purchased used, new, online, and from local supply houses.

Just as with equipment, the advantage of used is price and the downside may be less-than-perfect condition. For tables, you can purchase both the base and the table top individually online. This means you might find one used, say, table bases, and purchase new tops, giving you a new look and still saving money. For used chairs, particularly if they have primarily wood or metal rather than fabric surfaces, light refinishing may be an option. A light coat of a color-infused polyurethane will not only give you a nearly-new looking chair at a great price but it will also give you one that you can match perfectly to a similarly refinished table top or counter.

A quick way to familiarize yourself with an array of cost options for chairs and tables is to begin with eBay. You may not end there, but you will learn much about prices and options quickly.

POINT OF SALE (POS) SYSTEM

Depending on the volume of business your restaurant will transact and its serving style, it may be advantageous for you to use a point of sale (POS) system. For smaller operations a POS system may not be necessary. You will need to decide if purchasing or leasing one will offer an attractive rate of return on your investment, and if it does, how to prioritize that expenditure. Which system you select, and whether you lease or purchase the hardware, and whether your purchase or license the software, is an immensely complicated decision and one that, given the cost and impact on your business, should be extremely well-researched and well-considered. This is not a decision you will want to make based solely on the representations of one sales representative or supplier.

Switching to, or upgrading an existing POS system does not benefit all styles of restaurants equally. Table service restaurants report greater levels of satisfaction, particularly so with newer generations of systems that are mobile and allow tableside ordering and cashing out. Fast-casual restaurants report substantially lower levels of gains from instituting a POS systems.

POS systems can perform an array of functions depending on their price. It is helpful to talk about entry-level, mid-level, and high-level systems.

An **entry-level system**, and most older-generation systems, track sales, which allows you to determine peak sales volume times of day, to make same-hour, same-day, and same-week sales comparisons, to identify the quantity of each item sold (essential if you want to use the gross profit method of pricing), and to see sales averages for any period of time.

An entry-level system will allow you to see how much of each item is selling in any time period, which will allow you to calculate fairly precisely how much of each ingredient has been used and will need to be replaced, thereby simplifying your purchasing and making it more accurate.

Mid-level POS systems add to the above the ability to track labor and employees clocking in and out, and allows you to more accurately correlate the use of labor with sales volume, potentially reducing your cost of labor. Also, most systems in this price range can assist with reservations and seating, either using a proprietary system or integrating with opentable.com.

High-level systems typically have built-in inventory control where the system will continually update the available quantity of your stock as each order is placed, and will warn you of impending depletions, reducing the chance of a menu item being sold out. As well this sort of system can alert you to any unexplained shortages of high-value items such as alcohol, potentially decreasing inventory shrinkage from theft.

The focus of the newest generation of POS systems is mobility, allowing tableside ordering and payment processing, which can be a great labor saver for the server and a convenience for the customer. Newer systems are migrating from on-site installation to cloud-based deployment.

THINGS TO AVOID IN SELECTING A POS SYSTEM

Forced merchant services link: A number of POS systems only work with one merchant services (credit card processing) provider, the one associated with the POS system. It is very important for your long-term profitability that you negotiate the best possible deal for credit card processing, and if you are locked in to one particular processor because it is the only one your POS system is compatible with, you will have no leverage in the future in negotiating the best possible rate or in changing merchant services providers. By overpaying for merchant services every month, even if only by a fraction of a percentage, over the life of the POS system, you could effectively pay for it many times over. Avoid any POS system that locks you into a particular merchant services provider, even if appears the least-expensive option on the front end.

Linked software and hardware: Ideally the software and hardware components of a POS system should be independent; POS software should run on any computer or mobile device. Systems that are bundled with their own hardware should be avoided if you value your ability to easily make a change if the system does not work well for you.

Contract duration: There should be no need for a long-term contract to license POS software. Even without a lengthy contract, there is a strong disincentive for you to change POS systems (staff training, data migration, unfamiliarity, etc.), so a long-term commitment to any one POS vendor makes no sense for you. The more insistent a vendor is on a long-term contract, the more suspicious I become that they are struggling with customer dissatisfaction and retention issues. Happy customers have no incentive to change vendors.

CONSIDERATIONS WHEN SELECTING YOUR POS SYSTEM
Ease of use:

- Is the interface clear, easy to read, and intuitive. Does it fit with your menu? Is it easy to enter the menu item modifiers you typically use?
- How many actions does it take to ring up a simple transaction?
- Can you make live system or on-the-fly changes, eliminating out-of-stock items, or say adding a happy hour discount? If you have multiple stations, can you make changes from one that will populate in all?
- Can you easily create and add a menu item without having to create a button, add that button to your menu, and then connect the items in a multi-step process?

Intelligence and performance gathering ability: One of the most promising and intriguing ways that POS systems have evolved is in their collection of intelligence that can result in actionable insights, things you can better understand about your business and adjust to increase profitability. Examples of actionable insights afforded by a POS system might include: Which menu items are most and least profitable? Which types of customers are most and least valuable? What is the actual occupancy rate of your dining room? What is your average time per turnover?

Customer relationship management (CRM) potential: Newer-generation POS systems can harvest and store customers' email and phone numbers along with their order histories. They can send guests their receipts electronically and can retain data that can then be used to implement any sort of customer loyalty system you wish to put in place and to gain insight into your most profitable customers. The greater the amount of information you have, the greater the extent to which you can categorize or segment your most profitable customer groups. When it comes time to expand, that data – the demographic and psychographic characteristics of your most profitable customers – is gold.

Employee management potential: Many newer generation POS systems include a host of scheduling, time clock, and labor optimization tools. Specifically they can track employee hours, submit payroll directly from the system to the payroll processor, and in some instances predict staffing needs based on historical data.

Inventory control potential: State-of-the art systems track inventory depletion in real time, so as to avoid sold-out items, and can track raw materials from the time a shipment is received by the kitchen and, by knowing how much of each item is used for each menu item, track the accumulated use of each raw ingredient such that a manager can compare to a physical inventory to determine if there is theft or issues with portion control.

Menu firing: In some table-service operations it is useful if a server has the ability to hold an order and then to send to the kitchen when appropriate. This gives the server control over the order timing so that each course is prepared and delivered at the appropriate time.

Online ordering and reservations: Some systems allow the consumer to order or make reservations online directly, rather than relying on a third party.

Scalability: How much flexibility does the system have in terms of upgrades and expansions? Can you easily add additional stations as your business grows? What if you decide to add tableside ordering or online reservations? Are those features currently available?

Printing: There are two basic ways POS software handles the printing of the menu items. If the software prints based on the ticket itself, the entire ticket will be sent to one particular printer regardless of what it is. If the software prints based on the menu items, the alcohol would go to the bar and food would go to the kitchen, regardless of what is ordered on the ticket. Obviously, the latter setup is most ideal for a larger or more complex operation.

SELECTING A MERCHANT SERVICES PROVIDER

If you plan on accepting credit and debit cards, you will need a merchant services provider. There will be no shortage of providers seeking your business. In seeking proposals from different competing providers you may want to start with the bank handling your restaurant accounts. Many larger banks offer, or partner with providers of, merchant services and offer very competitive rates. National big box stores such as Costco and Sam's Club also partner with merchant services providers to offer these services to their members. Consider local independent providers too. Many are competitive in price and offer the additional advantage of in person "on-the-ground" support, which can be invaluable when trying to solve a processing issue during business hours.

The biggest difficulty in selecting a merchant services provider is determining an apples-to-apples basis of comparison that closely approximates what your actual charges will be. This is because credit card processing charges are based on a number of variables: the type of card processed, the average transaction size, the method of payment (in person vs. online), etc.

Don't be tempted by offers of free credit card terminals or other equipment. If you do, you will pay the value of the equipment many times over in higher processing and transaction fees. Best to reconcile yourself to purchasing a terminal and making the selection of a merchant services provider based on their fees charged for, as close as you can approximate it, the actual volume and type of credit cards you will be processing.

After selecting a merchant services provider and opening your doors for business, you will likely be approached by an onslaught of competing providers, each wishing to win over your business. My own experience is that, although many will promise substantial savings, when you actually sit down with them and go over your existing processors statements, if you have done a good job of selecting your initial processor, they will be unlikely to offer a meaningful savings, as merchant services providers are essentially intermediaries, all working with about the same cost structure.

SETTING YOUR HOURS OF OPERATION

What hours will you be open? This is a decision that can have a critical impact on your profitability, but is often made with little thought or analysis. A fair number of independent restaurants set hours of operation based on either the owner's personal time off preferences or some perception of what is normal and acceptable in the area. Both approaches are less than ideal.

Naturally throughout the day and week there will be an ebb and flow to your business, and consequently to your profitability. It behooves you to be open every day of the week and every hour of the day that is profitable and to be closed every hour that is not profitable. This logic though has to conform to the practicalities of managing staff and of the time and work required both to open the restaurant each day and to close it down at the end of the day.

Initially you can identify reasonable hours of operation based on your concept type and meals offered. Over time, by carefully monitoring sales on an hour-per-hour basis, you can experiment with cutting back or expanding hours. You may wish to do this seasonally.

SOME CONSIDERATIONS IN SETTING YOUR HOURS

Amortization of fixed costs: You have certain fixed costs, such as rent, equipment leasing, anything else that does not vary based on your business volume. The greater the amount of time you are open, the more days or hours per week, the more units (hours per day or days per week) that you have to amortize these costs over, the lower these costs per unit. For instance, if you are open five days per week, or 21 days per month on average, and your rent is $5,000 per month, your daily effective cost of rent is $238 per day. If, on the other hand, you were open seven days per week, or 30 days per month on average, your daily effective rent would be reduced to about $167 per day – a big difference.

Competition: It may make sense to be open hours when your competitors are closed. Many independent restaurants are closed on Monday. My restaurants are open seven days per week and Monday is one of our busiest weekdays, largely, I believe, because so many competing independent restaurants are closed on that day.

Demand: Let customer demand, not your preferred schedule, dictate hours of operation. You can always hire staff to work days when you prefer to be off. I am often surprised by coffee shop and breakfast-focused concept restaurants that are not open on Sunday. In the two of my restaurants that have a strong breakfast component, Sunday is not only our largest-grossing day of the week but, at La Waffleria, often has triple the sales volume of a weekday.

A PAUSE BEFORE OPENING

You may feel a great deal of pressure to open your doors as soon as possible after securing your final inspections and approvals from your local licensing authority. There is good reason to feel some urgency; until you are open you are paying for occupancy of your building or space with no offsetting income. As well there may be pressure from your staff who want to be productive and wage-earning as soon as possible. However, given all of the effort, money, and time that has lead up to this point combined with the necessity of getting it right, it may be a good time to actually pause for a moment. Consider scheduling an extra day or two make sure every piece of equipment, every system, is functioning just right before beginning your sequence of opening events.

Thirteen

Sourcing: where will you obtain all your supplies from?

S ourcing – finding suppliers for the food ingredients you will use for your various dishes, and for all other supplies and services you regularly use – will be an important factor in how well your restaurant does or doesn't do. The breadth of ingredients you are able to source impacts the breadth of the items you will be able to prepare. The quality and reliability of your suppliers enable you to, in turn, deliver high-quality dishes and to offer them without unintended interruption.

Your ability to source also will directly impact your bottom-line net profits. Overpaying by even a few percentage points can significantly erode profitability. And, how you source, whether products are delivered to your kitchen or whether you must go out and fetch them, will impact your available time.

SOURCING FOOD AND SUPPLIES
National purveyors: Most restaurants, including independents, source their core items from one of a handful of national restaurant distribution companies. This may be disappointing to hear. Wouldn't sourcing from one of the same national distributors that sell to the biggest name chain restaurants and franchises undermine the entire concept of local and independent?

It depends. If you are buying the same items that many chain and franchise restaurants buy – highly processed foods that are largely fully prepared and then frozen – then yes, it would likely reduce your restaurant's food quality to that of theirs. However, the majority of what all restaurant distributors offer are fairly straightforward raw ingredients, dairy, fresh fruits and vegetables, fresh meats, etc. So unless you are seeking specialized items such as organic, non-GMO, locally grown, or similar products, the large national distributors will likely be the best source for many of your core items.

One of the advantages of using a national restaurant supply company is the sheer breadth of items available, numbering into the tens of thousands, which can give you a near "one-stop shopping" experience. Another is that items are packed in a quantity per container with restaurants in mind, reducing redundant packaging. For most the biggest advantage of the big name national restaurant suppliers is their infrastructure for delivery directly to your kitchen. From their refrigerated tractor-trailers to "hot-shot" vans designed to deliver smaller quantities of an item you may have run out of, they excel at delivery.

The large national restaurant suppliers also offer a number of tools that can be of benefit. These range from online, or application-based ordering, software that links dynamic, real-time, food prices to your recipes such that you can see the cost of food for every menu item fluctuate in real time, and access to a host of industry-respected consultants and advisors.

Consider using one of the large national restaurant supply companies to provide the core, or bulk, of the supplies and ingredients you will need, unless your restaurant's focus is primarily on locally grown cuisine or on one particular ethnic type of fare.

Local and regional restaurant distribution companies: Local restaurant distribution companies can compete with the much larger national ones by carving out a niche for themselves, usually in a narrow food type. Local distributors may specialize in a particular ethnic type of restaurant, or in fresh fruits and vegetables, or in seafood. It is well worth investigating local restaurant suppliers. Generally they have great product knowledge, depth of product, and pricing within their narrowly defined niches.

You may find some regional suppliers who have some degree of vertical integration in their company, that is, that they own the means of production of some of the products they sell. For instance, I know of one that owns its own dairies in a neighboring state and is able to offer consistently lower prices on all dairy products. Suppliers who are able to utilize some degree of vertical integration to offer you consistently lower prices in certain product areas are worth seeking out.

Local: Many diners place a premium on locally raised produce, dairy, and meats. Many restaurant owners include some portion of their sourcing local for superior flavors, others do it with the goal of putting more money directly into their local economy, and other because it is a key aspect of their concept.

Local sourcing will impact your kitchen and menu, in that the products obtained directly from farmers and ranchers are, by definition, less processed. Most restaurants who source their meats locally primarily acquire whole-animal pork, chicken, goat, and sheep, which also helps offset the otherwise higher price associated with local sourcing. It may also make sense to purchase some items in season, locally, and then to preserve them by freezing and canning for later use.

If local sourcing is a significant part of your concept, you will need to develop a diverse number of relationships with individual farmers as each may have a few items that interest you, and that are currently in season. You can connect with area farmers through farmers markets and by noting the sourcing information from other restaurants in your area that utilize locally grown produce.

Tea: Do you have any local, well-respected, high-profile tea mixers and retailers? If so, you can leverage their reputation by carrying their teas, and storing and displaying bulk teas in containers branded with the local retailers variety-specific labels.

Coffee: Seek out local roasters. Typically your coffee will not be roasted until you place your order, insuring greater freshness. As well, if the roaster is known, you may be able to leverage their reputation, garnering greater coffee sales for your restaurant and greater exposure for the local roaster.

SOURCING SERVICES

Printing and signage: You may need printing services for paper or take-away menus, large display menus, forms, banners, and signage. What seems like an incidental expense may actually amount to a cost of several thousand dollars annually. Printing is an area where diligent shopping can save you from 50 to 80 percent of prices you would pay using the most casual source, such as "big box" office supply chains, which could be a significant addition to your annual bottom line.

For paper take-away menu printing, generally the most expensive choice is using copy shops associated with major national office supply chains. Try getting a bid from a locally owned independent copy shop. That alone can reduce the price by 30 to 50 percent. If the total number of copies involved are over several hundred, and particularly if the entire job is printed in black ink, get a bid from a local offset printer. Depending on the size of the job, this can further reduce the price by as much as 50 percent.

If you use custom-printed banners, get prices from a number of both online and local sources. We use lots of banners and by using a very high-volume, out-of-state, large-format printer, as compared to our nearest office supply store affiliated copy shop, and we save about 80 percent.

Large-size, full-color signage can be printed on sticky-backed stock and sent through the mail inexpensively. This opens up sourcing for your signage to a large number of online vendors. Custom neon signs can also be purchased through one of several specialized online manufacturers. We have neon at several restaurants and the cost we paid was almost exactly 50 percent of local quotes, including shipping.

Pest control: Local environmental health regulations will likely require monthly pest control treatment. Shop around and get estimates from both-brand name national franchises and local independent providers. In our case, by switching several restaurants at once to an independent local provider we were able to reduce our annual pest control expense by 50 percent as compared to the national brand-name provider we had been using.

Alarm monitoring: Hard-wired systems with third-party monitoring are still the norm in commercial buildings, but a new wave of internet-based systems, which can be self- or third-party monitored, are rapidly appearing. Even if you add on monthly third-party monitoring to a number of these internet-based monitoring systems, the monthly cost is still a fraction of that of the old hard-wired systems.

If you decide to stick with a traditional hard-wired system, avoid purchasing one connected with a monitoring company. This generally will lock you into a relationship with the monitoring division of the company, typically for an above-market price. Shop around and check out independent monitoring companies that are unaffiliated with alarm installation. That way, should you grow discontent with the monitoring service, you can easily switch providers.

There are a number of different internet-based security, smoke, and surveillance systems. Nest was one of the first to offer stand-alone smoke detectors that communicate through the internet with your smartphone.

They also offer single-camera surveillance systems that work the same way. SCOUT offers a well-reviewed wireless alarm system that you can self-monitor and have monitored by SCOUT itself. NOVI, iSmartAlarm, and SimpliSafe all offer component internet-based systems.

Given the impact of sourcing decisions, and relationships, on your bottom line, and ease of operations, be very thoughtful in researching and making your sourcing decisions. Think of sourcing, like so much else in the restaurant world, as a number of interrelated yet discreet ongoing relationships. Once sourcing decisions are made, revisit them frequently, comparing prices of like items between vendors.

Fourteen

Attracting, hiring, and keeping your ideal staff

Recruiting and retaining a top-notch staff, in both the front and back of the house, is critical to the success and smooth functioning of your restaurant. A customer's experience at your restaurant is very much a function of the quality of your staffing. A great staff will deliver wonderful service to your customers, will be highly productive, reliable, and invested. An ideal staff member will form and integral part of a dedicated, cohesive team.

A contented staff likely will lead to a low rate of turnover. Low turnover means less time spent recruiting and training new employees, and that individual employee's tenure will be sufficiently long for them to master their job and bond with the team.

The most helpful insight that I've had into restaurant staffing, the one that most changed my approach to hiring, is the realization that it is useful to categorize potential employees in one of two groups: the big fish and the small fish. For me the primary attribute of a big fish is stability. Whether it be from highly honed skills, a strong work ethic, an agreeable personality, stable life circumstances, or a combination of all of these things, big fish don't change jobs frequently, nor without good reason. They are valued by their employers and generally end up among the most highly paid in their workplace.

Conversely, small fish can be defined by their instability: frequent changes in employment, either from being terminated or from quitting. Their history of short tenures at each job may be a result of substance abuse (binge drinking seems epidemic in this industry), or a poor work ethic, or deep-seated personality issues (dishonesty, emotional volatility, etc.), or there may be purely situational issues (lack of reliable transportation, lack of child care, etc.), or there may be some combination of all of the above.

The advantage of hiring big fish is obvious; they are likely to stay with you in a way that is mutually satisfactory for a very long time.

Locating and hiring the small fish is easy. Because they end up unemployed so frequently they are often looking for employment, and may constitute the majority of those responding to an advertisement and applying for an opening. Locating and hiring the big fish is more difficult because they are seldom unemployed, and when they are, they are highly sought after. To effectively recruit the big fish you must develop a strategy of going to them, of identifying them and courting them before they leave their current job.

This may seem, and in many ways is, a vast over-simplification. People are complex and not easily, nor meaningfully, categorized by some binary system. Still, the underlying concept that the most valuable employees tend to be the most stable, and therefore worth recruiting, is very useful.

I began to realize how it is that the small fish form the bulk of available, job seeking, restaurant workers when I opened my second restaurant, La Waffleria. I placed a blind ad seeking line and prep cooks, only mentioning that we were a new restaurant and the neighborhood that we were located in. The first five respondents to the ad were each people whom I had previously dismissed from my first restaurant for unreliability and or poor performance! And, from their resumes, several of them had found, and lost, several other jobs in the intervening months.

How do you find these big fish, the super-dependable, those likely to work together with you as part of a team year after year? I usually find them through either their coworkers or prior coworkers. For those restaurant employees who have two jobs, working both for me and for another restaurant, I ask them who they work with at their other job who is a stellar performer and with whom they enjoy working. In the past, whom have they worked with who would be a great fit for our team? This works well as people are unlikely to recommend a former coworker who will not reflect well on them, and who is not dependable and with whom they are not comfortable working.

Once a big-fish target is identified, even if they are not looking for a job, I try to arrange for a meeting with them. My agenda in that meeting is primarily just to establish a relationship such that they will contact me first if they are contemplating a change. Beyond that, my goal is to attentively listen to them regarding any dissatisfaction they have with their current employment and to answer any questions they might have regarding my restaurants. There may be dissatisfactions that the person has for which I cannot offer an improvement (e.g., having to work early morning shifts, a pay rate that is already at the top of my compensation range, etc.). However, more often, what I hear is a sense that they are unappreciated, a lack of feeling part of a team, and a lack of feeling that they are part of something meaningful. I can tell them that they likely will have a very different experience as part of our team, and I can share with them some of the tangible things we do differently to make this the case. What is more effective, however, is when I invite them to interview my existing employees, particularly the one who connected me to them, and ask them about their experiences working for me. This often seals the deal.

Of course, not all people fit neatly into this big fish/small fish paradigm. We hire seasonal employees, and we hire people new to the restaurant business. Still though, using this "big fish only" targeted hiring strategy has been invaluable in creating a solid core of very reliable, high-achieving managers and senior staff.

INTERVIEWING

Whether interviewing a prospect that you've been attempting to recruit, or an applicant who has just walked in the door, work to make the most of the interview. You, the applicant, and perhaps one of your managers, should learn as much of relevance about each other as possible.

Conduct your interviews in a quiet spot, away from the noise and ears of a busy dining room. This allows for greater focus and comfort. Show respect for the applicant, and show what you expect from others, by being on time and giving the interview your undivided attention. Prepare ahead of time by reading the applicant's resume and highlighting areas you have questions about.

During the interview ask open-ended questions, particularly ones that allow the prospect to express their own thinking and experiences regarding customer service, such as, "Describe the sequence of events from a customer entering the building to leaving that might result in that customer having an ideal experience."

Note the details. Is the applicant's dress appropriate for the position (erring toward formal is okay; erring toward informal, less so). Does their posture indicate they are attentive and engaged? Are there unexplained gaps in their employment?

It is helpful to have in mind a closing for the interview. Thank the applicant for their time and give them a period of time within which you will contact them and specify how you will do so.

In my restaurants, if after reviewing their resume, checking their references, and interviewing them, we are seriously interested in an applicant, we will invite them for a one-day (paid) working interview. The working interview tells us much that would never be uncovered in a sitting interview. What is the applicant's physical intelligence (do they move in the kitchen with efficiency and surety or are they inefficient or clumsy in their movements)? How do they physically interact in a busy kitchen or dining room (are they aware of the movements of others and able to seamlessly integrate or are they frequently colliding with people)? Have they taken the initiative to prepare for the day by familiarizing themselves with the menu? How strong is their ability to memorize? Are they naturally at ease around, and friendly with, customers or do they come off as stiff and reticent?

We have had applicants that had a great resume and shone in their verbal interview but did poorly on their working interview and we have had the opposite, applicants that seemed unimpressive during their verbal interview but just blew us away with their physical intelligence and ability to physically navigate a crowded kitchen during their working interview. It is difficult to know how someone will function on the job until you see them in action.

ATTRACTING THE BEST
It is important to think about the employee/employer dynamic from the perspective of the prospective employee. Why would a talented kitchen manager, cook, barista, or server want to work for your restaurant as compared to one of your competitors? If you want to attract and retain the best, it is important to clearly and accurately understand what your competitors are offering, and how that compares to what you can offer. This is not limited to compensation; it also includes benefits, recognition, sense of purpose, sense of team, and many other subtle tangible and intangible variables that make it more or less rewarding to work for a given restaurant.

Compensation: One of the factors that has allowed us to attract and retain some of the best staff is our approach to tip distribution. Most of our competitors pay the front of the house (servers, cashiers, baristas, food runners, etc.) the federal minimum wage for tipped employees and rely on the tips to boost the front of the house employee earnings to minimum wage. The back of the house staff (line cooks, prep cooks, etc.) then, are paid a higher fixed hourly wage and receive no tips.

It occurred to me very early in owning restaurants that this standard arrangement has the potential to be inherently divisive, and does not reflect the reality of how mutually dependent each portion of the team is on the other. Customer satisfaction, and thus tips, is dependent upon the efforts of both sides of the house (if your food quality is poor and your wait time excessive, you are less likely to tip). I made the decision to pay all employees an hourly wage that was well-above minimum wage and to institute a policy that all tips would be split equally between front of the house and back of the house employees. I instituted this policy four years ago, now employ it in three different restaurants, and consider it a factor in both our very low employee turnover and our ability to successfully recruit best-of-the-best employees. Of course, there is no "free lunch" or in this case, free money. Paying employees more costs me more. I calculate that my labor as a percentage of gross sales is likely 2 to 3 percent higher than were I using a more conventional compensation system. This additional cost of labor comes directly from each restaurant's bottom-line earnings. For me, however, this modest reduction in our net earnings is well worth the improvement in my quality of life that having a very low rate of turnover (which saves much time in interviews, hiring, and training) affords and the enhanced service and product quality that we are able to deliver. It also gives me an edge in recruiting and retaining the best employees.

ENLIST THE HELP OF YOUR FANS

Among those regular customers who adore your restaurant may be your next great employee. I have found that people who love to dine out and who love our restaurant's concepts, culture, and quirkiness often have an interest in working for us. Other potential great employees are those who are drawn to you personally, through prior experience having formed a positive opinion of you. A great way to reach out to both categories, fans of the restaurant and fans of you, is Facebook. Some of my best employees have come from posting openings on both the restaurant's and on my own Facebook page. Other social media, particularly Twitter and Instagram, can be deployed similarly. As well, any job openings can be posted on your restaurant's website.

If the scale of your operation warrants it, you may wish to have a permanent "work for us" page on your web site which lists some of the advantages and benefits of working for you such as "paid vacation after first year, 401(k) program, etc.". You may want to use tags such as "Line Cook Wanted" and post actual job openings so that the page is picked up by search engines in searches by local job seekers.

ESTABLISHING THE WORK CULTURE AT YOUR RESTAURANT

It is worth giving some thought to the sort of work culture that you want to establish and maintain in your restaurant. Traditionally, many restaurants have given themselves license to maintain a harsh, acerbic, culture characterized by managers and chefs flying into rages, frequent emotional outbursts, on-the-spot dismissals, and pans being hurled across the kitchen. It should go without saying that allowing this sort of toxic environment is counterproductive to potentially every goal you might have for your restaurant culture: it creates tension rather than comfort; it makes working at your restaurant a miserable experience; it undermines team cohesion; and it can cost you some of your best employees. And your customers may be much more tuned in to the workplace dynamics than you think, and will pick up on a tense, unhappy environment. It would seem obvious that this sort of unpleasant work culture should be avoided at all costs. However, because at one time it was so pervasive in the restaurant business, there is still a legacy of it today, a minority of chefs or managers who think it is permissible, or even expected. Prevent this by first leading by example and secondly by making it unambiguously clear that you will not tolerate mean, abusive, inappropriate behavior.

RETAINING STAFF

While there will always be some organic turnover, employees moving out of town, or making an educational or career change, the loss of a valued employee because of preventable or solvable dissatisfaction is a sad and costly thing. I hear a range of employee dissatisfactions, mostly from recruiting high-performing employees from other restaurants.

Assuming you are paying employees fairly at or slightly above market for their capabilities, you will rarely lose employees solely based on compensation, unless they are transitioning into a field that pays substantially more than restaurant work.

In recruiting employees from my competitors, the complaints I most often hear relate to the employee feeling unappreciated or disrespected. One of my superstar cooks mentioned, at the job I recruited her away from, working in a two-cook kitchen, having the second cook fail to show up, and rather than finding a second cook, or even rolling up their sleeves and stepping into the kitchen themselves, management left her as the single cook for an entire day. Being super-capable, she was able to keep up but the experience left her feeling bitter and, after 10 years in the same kitchen, ready for a change. The lesson? Show consideration for your people, don't put them in a position to endure unusual hardship, and if you have to, acknowledge it and find a way to make it right.

It surprises me how often employees, in explaining why they left their last job, say something like, "I didn't feel any purpose. I just felt like some part of a giant machine." Almost everyone one wants some sense of purpose and achievement in their work. You can go a long way toward providing this through encouraging buy-in with the restaurant concept, with the restaurant's level of performance, and with positive reviews. Also, individual acknowledgement and sincere expressions and demonstrations of appreciation will go a long way to help with this. There are hundreds of ways to do this and you will find ways that are congruous with your personality and values.

The right staffing can make the difference in your experience of owning a restaurant from one that is characterized by constant struggle, turmoil, and disappointment to one that is characterized by comradery, predictability, shared hard work, and shared joy.

Fifteen

Orchestrating the opening of your restaurant

BEFORE YOU SET AN OPENING DATE

Why not make your first day in business your grand opening? Certainly many restaurants do this. However, many restaurants, particularly innovative, independent ones, have very publicly disastrous grand openings, discovering critical production and staffing issues only when everything falls apart on their opening day. I believe in most cases, where your restaurant is not an exact clone of a previous one you have opened, it makes more sense to approach the process gradually, in several well-defined steps, each with its own objectives.

PHASE ONE: A TASTING PARTY

The idea of this very preliminary and tentative soft opening is to test your recipes on the public, to test your cook's ability to reliably produce your menu items, and to give servers familiarity and practice with presenting your menu items.

A Phase One soft opening can be thought of as a tasting party. The guests are friends, friends of your staff, business associates – in short, a friendly, yet honest audience. Avoid inviting press and celebrities at this point.

Food can be delivered family-style, so that each guest gets to taste multiple items. At this stage you may wish to present only a handful of menu items, so as to keep the focus on the mainstay items, the core of your menu.

You may ask your guests to complete a survey card, scoring and rating each of your menu items, or you may initiate a less-formal group discussion about each item.

This sort of opening allows you to reconsider any items that receive consistently poor reviews or that turn out to be onerous to produce, and to modify others based on the feedback you receive.

A Phase One soft opening is an initial run-through, a dress rehearsal, with a live audience, but with many of the components of the process such as placing orders, fulfilling orders, and processing payment, etc. temporarily removed. Your Phase One opening should be a fun affair for you and your staff that also serves to illuminate any food-production and food-quality problems.

PHASE TWO: PRODUCING ALL ITEMS TO ORDER

After addressing any issues that arose with menu items and production in Phase One, plan a second soft opening a week or so later. In this one you will launch all items on the menu, and items will be cooked to order.

You may expand the group of people you invite, perhaps making it more professional and less personal. You might invite business associates, customers, supporters, owners of neighboring businesses, etc.

The systems that will be tested here are: the ability of the order taker to take the order and, either by hand or with your POS system, create a ticket for the kitchen, the kitchen's ability to correctly read the ticket and prepare the requested dish in a timely fashion and to plate it appropriately, and the server's ability to deliver and present each dish.

The components of the system that you have not yet introduced, and won't yet be testing, are your restaurant's ability to produce menu items at high volume, under pressure, and the financial part of the transaction. You control the order volume by the number of people that you invite. The idea here is to mimic low-volume conditions rather than the very high-volume, high-stress, conditions that you might encounter during an actual grand opening.

In lieu of charging for each dish, you may consider making the event free for your guests and encourage tipping or you might ask for a donation at the door to a specified charity or cause.

The primary idea here is to allow staff to work in real-life conditions without them being overwhelmed by an onslaught of customers and to identify any issues that arise under these controlled conditions and to make adjustments accordingly.

PHASE THREE: A QUIET OPENING

After making adjustments in response to any issues that arose in your Phase Two opening, it is time to bring the last piece of your operations into the picture: the transactional component. Schedule several hours of time with your cashiers during which they can practice ringing up mock orders and explaining menu items and answering potential customer questions. Make sure they are completely comfortable with the POS system and other equipment they will be using to complete transactions.

In Phase Three you open with full functionality, but without a great deal of fanfare or buildup. This allows all staff to practice all aspects of their positions without the pressure of high volume of business, possible media scrutiny, and the drama of an opening night production. The opening may, to the public, appear quite sudden and with little publicity. Those that find their way to it will likely do so by accident, stumbling over it, rather than due to your promotion. It may even take many people in your trade area some time to even notice that you are open for business. This is all intentional. You will have many other opportunities for publicity, fanfare, drama, and doing a lucrative high-volume of business. Use this time to hone your team's skills, increase their confidence, and ferret out any remaining production or quality issues that need to be addressed.

PHASE FOUR: YOUR GRAND OPENING

I suggest planning your grand opening for two weeks or so after you have been open and in operation. You will have used the weeks prior to your grand opening to perfect every aspect of your operation from order taking through food delivery. If there are any unacceptably weak links in your staff, you will have made corrections or changes. Also, you and your staff will be relaxed and at the top of your game, and likely enjoy your grand opening, rather than it being a tense and risky affair.

Free press for your opening: In most markets, the opening of a new restaurant, particularly a local, independent, and novel one, is newsworthy.

When I opened La Wafflería, my all-waffle restaurant, we were featured on one local news program days before we actually opened, and shortly after opening, we were invited to prepare some of our dishes live on a local morning news program. We've also had articles on us appear in local magazines and weeklies nearly a dozen times in our first year. All of this publicity was enormously valuable, and has never cost us anything. I attribute it to the fact that we make for an interesting story; an all-waffle restaurant located in a nearly 100-year-old house, with a non-stop line of customers.

It is well worth your time to develop a strategy to maximize free publicity for your grand opening and for the months following. Begin by thinking not like a restaurant entrepreneur but like a reporter. What would make this story interesting to readers or viewers? An interesting backstory helps. How did you come to open a restaurant? What was your prior career? What was the catalyst to getting into the restaurant business? Is your food concept novel? Do you have compelling, high-resolution photographs of your food? Is your building historic, novel, or otherwise interesting? If you can develop a few quotable, succinct sentences that express your concept, story, or whatever else would be interesting to viewers or readers it will go a long way toward garnering you publicity. Remember, the fact that you are very excited about your new restaurant and would like free publicity means nothing to a reporter. Having something that the reporter believes would make for an interesting, fun, attention-grabbing, story is everything.

Assemble a press package that includes a press release that is concise, compelling, well-written, and clearly focused on those things that would make your restaurant newsworthy. Have a professional photographer (or a friend with a good camera) take some high-quality photos of a few of your most photogenic offerings. You can email prints with your publicity package but most importantly, indicate that "high resolution digital files available upon request." For a budget-minded editor or producer, not having to dispatch a photographer can give your story an edge over another competing one.

Take the various phases of your opening slowly. Most restaurant owners feel pressure to get the doors open and to have money coming in but, to use a cliché, you have only one chance to make a good first impression. Take the time, build up to your grand opening gradually making adjustments along the way, and enjoy the experience.

Sixteen

Marketing your restaurant creatively and cost-effectively

THE RELATIONSHIP BETWEEN THE PERCEIVED VALUE OF AN OFFER AND THE COST-EFFECTIVENESS OF MARKETING IT

Before talking much about avenues and techniques available for marketing and promoting your restaurant, let's take a moment and look at the interplay between the perceived value of any offering and how that perception affects our rate of return on your advertising dollar. Take the example of a piece of real estate. It could be priced at any point along a continuum with, at one end, a price that is clearly and substantially below market, maybe a fraction of its market value, and on the other end, a price that is substantially above market value, maybe many times the market value of the item. On the underpriced end of the spectrum, the property would sell very quickly, likely to the first person who found out about it and had the means to purchase it. The fact that the property was underpriced would be so evident that no advertising would be necessary in order to quickly sell it. On the overpriced end of the continuum, we could spend a fortune advertising it, and still no one would purchase it. Any money spend advertising it would have generated no return on investment our and would have been a complete waste.

The above is a simplistic example, but it underlines the fact that clearly there is a relationship between the perceived value of an offer and the cost-effectiveness of marketing it. It makes no sense to market something that is perceived to be overpriced or has very little appeal at any price. Money spent advertising an offer with low perceived value is likely to be wasted money. You cannot advertise your way out of lack of sales due to your offerings being perceived as offering a poor value for the price. Advertising is no magic bullet.

Of course underpricing is not profitable either. There is a sweet spot, an ideal price that is profitable for the seller but also sufficiently compelling to the customer so as to achieve maximum return on your advertising dollar. Once you are able to deliver a product that is in demand at the price you are asking for it, advertising can be invaluable in bringing your restaurant to, and helping it maintain, its full productive capacity.

AN OVERALL STRATEGY: BUILDING A COALITION OF CUSTOMERS

Most successful politicians win elections by building coalitions. They assemble discrete groups of voters who are strongly motivated by one particular issue with groups motivated by another different issue into larger groups of supporters. This works as long as the issues that motivate each group are not mutually exclusive. Similarly, many restaurants achieve success by developing discrete followings or constituencies that together form a large group of customers. In politics as well as restaurants, it is often more effective to tailor your advertising to the passions of distinct groups than it is to deliver a very generic message to a much larger group.

At Tia Betty Blue's, we have several very diverse customer groups that exist within our trade area including: aficionados of traditional northern New Mexico cuisine (our specialty), Air Force personnel (we are blocks from a large Air Force base), people on restrictive diets (we've always offered vegetarian, vegan, and gluten-free versions of most of our most popular dishes). In our advertising, and messaging, we often approach each group separately, with completely different messages.

NO-COST PROMOTION

There are many ways to effectively promote your restaurant that do not require a cash outlay. Let's examine those before moving on to more costly alternatives.

GETTING FAVORABLE PRINT AND BROADCAST REVIEWS

In the preceding chapter on orchestrating your opening, we cover securing free publicity for your opening and for your first month or so in business. Realize that garnering publicity for your opening is a very different task than getting reporters and food bloggers to review your restaurant on an ongoing basis. First of all, many publications are in no hurry to dispatch a reviewer. Many have had the experience of reviewing a just-opened restaurant only to have it fail in the first month or so. It may take several months for local restaurant reviews to become convinced that you will be around for a while and worth writing about.

A good place to begin in seeking published professional reviews on your restaurant is with reaching out to local food bloggers. Find out who the big names are in local food and restaurant review blogs, contact them, and offer to send them a free gift certificate to your restaurant. Many prominent bloggers have large followings of people who take food seriously, and a few positive reviews can gain you many new customers. As well, food bloggers seem to function as a sort of vanguard, reviewing new places first before print and broadcast reporters get to it. I suspect many print and broadcast reporters rely on bloggers to locate new and interesting restaurants to review so getting reviewed by some of your better-followed local food bloggers can be a necessary first step.

Pay attention to who your local print food reviewers are, both for the newspaper and alternative weekly publications. Email them, invite them to your restaurant, send them a few enticing photos, and in only a paragraph or so, explain your concept and something that makes it unique, interesting, and most importantly, newsworthy.

Restaurants, particularly if newish, and if they have some interesting story, can make compelling stories for locally produced morning news shows. From the station's website, or by calling, find out who the producer of each local morning show is, write them a brief email offering your establishment for a segment, and include the most interesting aspects of your story or the restaurant's concept and several photos of the most interesting dishes and of the restaurant's interior and exterior.

Some locally produced morning shows feature in-studio cooking where you and or one of your cooks are interviewed and filmed live actually preparing a dish your restaurant features. If your market has such a program, and you have a dish that can be prepared in a cooking show context, contact the producer and share your story with them and suggest a dish you think would work for their show. Include photos. Consider the story from the producer's point of view and suggest what would make it of particular interest to their viewers.

CROWD-SOURCED REVIEWS

Likely the impact on your business from ongoing crowd-sourced reviews – Yelp, Google+, Urban Spoon, Trip Advisor, and similar – will be far greater than the impact from professionally written online, print, or broadcast reviews. This is true for several reasons. Crowd-sourced reviews are constant, a background phenomenon, always there, from shortly after you open until as long as you are in business. Print and broadcast reviews are one-time events. They make a splash and then quickly fade away.

More importantly, crowd-sourced reviews are more likely to be relevant to the person encountering them than print or broadcast reviews. A given restaurant's trade area, the geographic area that accounts for the vast majority of its business, is relatively small, often a mile or so in diameter. The size of the area over which a broadcasts will be heard, or a print publications distributed, are giant by comparison. Thus a review of your restaurant will be largely irrelevant to the vast majority of the readers or viewers who encounter it, as they will likely not live close enough to your restaurant to frequent it. Geography aside, a broadcast or print review may be irrelevant from the standpoint of preference as well; the specific type of food may be well outside of the reader's or viewer's preferences and therefore of no interest to them.

A crowd-sourced review, on the other hand, is likely to be encountered by a potential customer when they are either looking for options nearby or are looking for a certain genre of food, or both, making reviews about your restaurant suddenly extremely relevant to them. And they are usually hungry, further increasing the relevance into something like an urgency.

Crowd-sourced reviews are a double-edged sword, with the potential to equally attract or repel customers. For crowd-sourced reviews to have a beneficial impact, they must be overwhelmingly positive and reflect high customer ratings.

Given that over 80 percent of restaurant patrons nationally say that they research a restaurant online before visiting it, positive crowd-sourced reviews are critical to the success of your restaurant. So, how can you best manage them? There may be the temptation, particularly after reading negative, inaccurate, or unfair reviews, to want to simply opt out, to ignore the entire phenomenon. Unfortunately, that is not an option. Crowd-sourced reviews continue to accumulate, and people will be guided by them, whether you pay attention to them or not, or whether you respond to them or not. Worse than simply ignoring them is responding with anger or defensiveness. It is tempting, as some percentage will be wildly inaccurate, make grossly unfair generalizations, or be outright dishonest. However, expressing anger in response only makes you look hostile.

To be able to manage crowd-sourced reviews for both Yelp and Google+, you will want to claim your business page as soon as you open your doors. For Google+ you will create a Google account, find your business, select "Manage this page," and proceed to enter your business location, hours, and photos. Google will validate your listing either by phone (at the phone number registered to the business) or by sending a card to the business address. The process with Yelp is similar. Going through this process allows you to claim and then manage your restaurant's listing.

Check crowd-sourced review sites regularly and respond to both positive and negative comments quickly. A response to a negative review should always begin with an apology to the consumer for the bad experience that they had. This can be sincerely done no matter how outrageous or inaccurate the negative review may be because, as restaurant owners, we do honestly wish that the customer had had a positive experience. Then you can address the particular complaint and briefly explain what your plan is to correct the situation, if that is appropriate. For example "We are sorry that you found service too slow on your visit. Providing prompt service at all times of day is important to us. Our business has recently picked up during that time period and we are in the process of adding to our staffing for that shift." Or, "We are sorry that during your visit you found the bathroom to be untidy. We take this seriously and are working on an hourly checklist to use to insure that bathroom cleanliness is frequently monitored by our staff." If the complaint involves a dissatisfaction where the customer did not get full value for their money, for instance an item was not received or was disappointing, it can be good to ask the customer to contact you so that you can "make it right." A credit or gift certificate is a small price to pay to retain a customer that would otherwise be lost forever. Finally, ask the customer back with a simple "We are really sorry about that and hope you will give us another try." Remember that the larger audience is not the disgruntled patron but rather the many more people who are reading reviews and deciding whether or not to visit your restaurant for the first time.

You should respond equally quickly to positive reviews. Take the time to thank them. Creating a connection with these fans helps spread word-of-mouth buzz and benefits your online reputation.

There may be a temptation to try to game the system in various ways, say by offering a discount to anyone who writes a positive review. It is best not to go down this road. Your good food, value proposition, great service, and sincerity will be enough to earn favorable reviews so there is no need to try to stack the deck. Also, though often exaggerated, negative reviews often do contain some grain of truth and can provide valuable insight into what is working and what isn't.

SOCIAL MEDIA

Your restaurant will have a social media presence whether you are involved in it or not. Your customers will be posting to Facebook, tweeting, and uploading Instagram photos and these posts and tweets will be seen by thousands. That being the case, it makes sense to use social media to your advantage.

The "social" aspect of social media is lost on many. Much like a conversation, it is best not thought of as a one-way street. Your use of social media should not be exclusively about promoting specials or encouraging visits to your restaurant. Try for a mix of engagement posts, those things you post solely because they will be of interest to your followers, and conversion posts, which encourage the views to take action. An engagement post might be of a recipe, an interesting occurrence at your restaurant, or anything that is relevant and redeems itself in entertainment value. A promotional post, on the other hand, promotes a specific offer or special.

As with crowd-sourced review sites, you should respond to comments on social media platforms, both positive and negative ones, promptly and positively.

Be sure that your bio or profile for each social media account has your address and hours of operation so that people can click through to quickly get this information. Facebook lets you also include your hours of operation, phone number, and website in your profile. Instagram bios can also include your restaurant address and hours.

Making some offers available only to those who follow you on social media will give those customers a good reason to continue to engage with your posts. Value offers don't always have to revolve around a steep discount. Giving followers first notice of a new menu item or daily special also attracts interest and may have value to them.

For Twitter and Instagram, make use of popular and trending hashtags. Extend the reach of your food photo posts by adding the appropriate hashtags such as #waffles, #gelato, or #vegan. Also use hashtags for each photo with your city or neighborhood.

PAID ADVERTISING

As a new restaurant owner you will be besieged by armies of salespeople who will try to sell you on every conceivable type of advertising and promotion including print ads, search engine optimization, custom mobile apps, emblazoned caps, and requests for team sponsorships. It makes sense to think through an advertising strategy, and to have an advertising budget set in advance, rather than considering each "opportunity" in a vacuum.

EXPOSURES VS. USEFUL EXPOSURES

The basic unit that advertising is sold by, whether explicitly stated or not, is the number of people who will see the ad, or at least be exposed to it. In a print publication this might be the circulation of the publication; in a broadcast this may be the number of listeners or viewers the station has at a given time of day. However, it is critically important to remember that the vast majority of those exposures – whether they are to magazine or newspaper readers, television viewers, or radio listeners, or to readers of some restaurant-related website – will be of no benefit to you because the person viewing the ad is not a potential customer. This will be the case because they do not live in or near your trade area or do not have an affinity for the exact food, or restaurant concept, you offer. For example, if a given local publication boasts a circulation of 100,000 but, based on the distribution of their subscribers, you determine that only about 1 percent are in your trade area, than you can assume that your ad will be seen by about 1,000 people who have any probability of becoming regular customers.

A multi-store restaurant, on the other hand, with stores distributed throughout the entire area over which a publication is distributed, or a broadcast is heard, could potentially benefit from all 100,000 people reading the publication and thus would get full value for their advertising buy. Your one store, benefiting from only 1 percent of the readers, would effectively be paying 100 times more per meaningful exposure, likely way more than could be justified by the potential increase in sales. So, when considering an advertising expenditure, always calculate the real cost to you per relevant exposure, based on the percentage of readers, viewers, or listeners who are actually in a position to be motivated to act by the ad.

CALCULATING THE RETURN ON YOUR ADVERTISING EXPENDITURES

Most discussions of advertising for restaurants, and all that I have seen online, neglect an essential question: how do you know if you are losing money, breaking even, or making a positive return on a potential advertising expenditure? Advertising sales people I've encountered all seem to believe that return on advertising expense is something to be taken for granted, or vaguely grasped experientially, rather than measured and analyzed from a cost benefit perspective.

If you spend a dollar on advertising, how much business must that advertising bring in to break even or earn a return on your advertising investment? This depends on your net profit margin (the percentage of every dollar that you retain after all expenses). If you operate at a 10 percent net profit margin, and $1 spent on advertising increases your business by $1, then you have lost 90 percent, or 90 cents for each dollar you spend on the ad buy. Just to break even on the advertising buy, if your net profit margin is 10 percent, every dollar spent on advertising would need to generate $10 in new sales. Of course this is simplistic and neglects the long-term value to you of the percentage of new customers who become repeat customers, and it neglects some other potential long-term gains such as building brand awareness. Still, it does give you a rough benchmark to use in evaluating your return on investment in any advertising program.

NEWSPAPER, MAGAZINE, BROADCAST AND OTHER "LARGE REACH" ADVERTISING

As we have discussed, very large-reach media such as television, cable television, newspapers, and magazines will generally have a reach so much larger than the trade area of your restaurant that, for a single-store independent business, they generally cannot deliver relevant exposures at a price that would lead to a positive return on your advertising dollar.

On the other hand, using small-reach publications, such as advertising in a university newspaper when your restaurant is adjacent to a campus and the entire campus is in your trade area, or on a radio program that caters to an ethnicity for whom you are one of the few restaurants to offer their cuisine, may generate a high rate of return on your advertising dollar.

To calculate your return on your advertising dollar, you will need to be able to segregate and measure business directly attributable to the advertising campaign from your normal, pre-advertising, business. For print advertising, coupons are a traditional way of doing this but may not be convenient for the customer or feel compatible with your business image. Asking customers in your ad to mention the publication the ad appears in in order to receive the advertised discount or premium may help you track the ad's performance but only if you and your staff have an accurate way of tallying this information.

TARGETED DIRECT MAIL

Traditional bulk mail, sending many mailers to a mailing list that you have purchased or assembled, is still relatively expensive per piece and time-consuming to process. There is a relatively new type of bulk mail called EDDM (Every Door Direct Mail) which costs much less, requires very little time to process, and is ideal for restaurants who have and know the boundaries of their trade area.

EDDM mailers are delivered to every address in a letter carrier route, rather than being individually addressed. Using the free online tools that the United States Postal Service provides, you can select individual postal carrier routes that may have from just over a hundred residents to just under a thousand. You can add routes until you have covered your entire trade area, or you can have it delivered to the carrier routes that only contain people most likely to become your customers. You can exclude any carrier routes that you believe would give you a low response rate based on demographics or traffic patterns and you can select that your mailing exclude business, or apartment residents, if you like. EDDM pieces cost roughly half of that of traditional sorted bulk mail pieces to send because they require virtually no sorting by the post office. You simply print off identifying information for each route, bundle them by route, and drop the mailing off at your local post office. And, unlike traditional bulk mail which penalizes you for large-sized pieces, EDDM allows an oversized mailer at no additional charge.

In the first years of my restaurant Tia Betty Blue's we used EDDM extensively to build up a following in several pockets within our trade area and were able to verify a great return on our ad dollars.

TRADE AND BARTER

What is interesting about barter transactions is that you trade meals or gift certificates for something that you would have otherwise had to pay for in cash. If your restaurant has excess capacity, unfilled seats, it may make sense to use barter to utilize your restaurant's excess capacity.

At all of my restaurants we almost never pay cash for advertising. We prefer to trade food (in the form of gift certificates) for it. One weekly tabloid that we work with sells gift certificates for our restaurant online and credits us with the value against our advertising. Thus, rather than paying for advertising out of a portion of our bottom line profits we pay for them by selling more meals, hopefully to new customers.

With any advertising proposal my first question is always about relevance and return on my investment: Are the people for whom I am paying to see the ad statistically likely to become regular customers? My second question, if I like the answer to the first, is, Can we work out a trade?

ONLINE ADVERTISING

There are innumerable opportunities to spend money for online advertising that will likely yield very little to no return on your advertising dollar. And some of the most cost-effective and easily targeted and tracked advertising also takes place online.

To begin to separate the wheat from the chaff, take a look at how you go about selecting a restaurant, particularly in unfamiliar surroundings. Do you browse through many individual restaurant websites, investigating each? Do you use some third-party restaurant advertising portal? Do you rely primarily on crowd-sourced review sites and start by examining restaurants in a certain price range nearest to you, or perhaps of a certain type of cuisine that you are in the mood for? I suspect it is the latter.

That being the case, why would you pay for "Search Engine Optimization" to make your website appear slightly higher than some other restaurant's in a generic Google search when few people go about finding a place to eat in that way? Why would you pay to list your restaurant in some third-party restaurant portal site that features a carelessly assembled list of every restaurant (or business with the word restaurant in their name) clearly scraped from some public records, when no one would actually go about finding a place to eat at in this way?

Similarly, why would you pay someone to develop a custom mobile restaurant app when there are several very popular apps for crowd-sourced review based sites that work extremely well, and are popular and free?

What class of online advertising is cost-effective? We have had wonderful results with various social media sites and have been able to clearly and narrowly target ads to our exact target audience, and to measure response and analyze the return on our advertising dollar.

FACEBOOK PAID ADVERTISING
Begin by constructing a Facebook page for your restaurant and asking existing customers to "like" it. It helps if you give them a reason to do so, such as exclusive access to offers and promotions. The larger the group who has "liked" your page the greater the number of people who you can engage with via posts to your page and who, most likely, already have familiarity with your establishment. As well, encourage guests to "check in" on Facebook from your restaurant. When customers do this, the post is shared with all of their friends. The average Facebook user has 245 friends, so this friend-to-friend boosting can be extremely beneficial.

However, they may or may not organically (i.e., without you paying to promote it) see your post in their newsfeed, depending on the nuances of the particular algorithm Facebook uses. There are several types of paid advertising available on Facebook. By far the most useful for a restaurant owner is the promoted post feature wherein a photo, typically a photo of an appealing special, is posted along with a description of the offer. Be sure to include your restaurant's address at the end of the post, as many people many not click through to your page but you still want them to know where you are. You can increase the people for whom this ad will appear in their newsfeed by "boosting" it, that is, paying an amount of money that you select for a given number of exposures. You can then select your target audience based on their location, age, social connection to anyone who has already "liked" the page, or other demographics. We find that with this sort of advertising, which gives us a high level of control of who sees the ad, we are able to achieve great relevance of our posts to the potential customer and consequently a high return on our advertising dollar.

GUERILLA MARKETING

Guerilla marketing is the sort of advertising that is high on imagination and low on cost. It employees creative, often totally audacious, sometimes legally iffy, techniques. Guerilla marketing can be a sling shot in the hands of a David, a great weapon in the arsenal of a new independent restaurant.

When I opened Tia Betty Blue's, although we bordered a busy arterial street, which provided access to a Veterans Administration hospital, and an Air Force base, because our building was set back from the street and looked nothing like a restaurant, few people seemed to notice us. I hired various neighborhood characters to stand on the sidewalk in front of our place during rush hour, and hold up a large sign advertising various specials that we offered. We rotated the messages frequently, noting which ones worked best. This brought in the people we most wanted, people on their way to work, or leaving work to find a spot for lunch. Years later, many of the customers our "signers" brought in are still regulars.

Another guerilla marketing technique that I used in our first year was to offer a very generous discount (30 percent!) to people who worked for various employers in our trade area, but only on one specific day per week per group. For instance, on Mondays we offered the discount to educators as there were several schools nearby, on Tuesdays we offered it to veterans and anyone working at the nearby Air Force base, etc. Probably the kookiest was our Friday discount, where anyone who had a visible tattoo got the 30 percent discount. The occupation-based discounts were useful in attracting groups of people who worked together. My intent was that someone on the Air Force base, in a discussion with their coworkers one Tuesday about where to have lunch, would volunteer that if they all went to Tia Betty's for lunch they could all save 30 percent, which would be enough to incentivize the group to try our otherwise unknown restaurant. Our sign holders advertised the discount of the day, catching the eye of motorists on their way to work in for large employers in our market area.

Word of our very quirky visible tattoo discount day seemed to spread naturally and quickly but I helped it along with cards that I hand-delivered to various tattoo studios near our restaurant, explained to the owners, and offered to post their advertising on our bulletin board in return. It didn't take long until nearly every seat in the house was filled every Friday with people sporting visible tattoos.

A discount this large would generally not be sustainable from a profitability standpoint, and we discontinued it after our first year. However, it served its purpose in getting us established with the people that mattered most to us, those living in or working in our trade area.

We also used temporary tattoos to publicize Tia Betty's. Kids love them and pictures of cute kids sporting your logo are a nice addition to our online advertising.

A common guerilla marketing technique is to always carry a simple business card with some sort of offer or discount on it that the person you give the card to can take advantage of. The card need only contain the restaurant name, address, website, and offer, something such as "This card good for a 20 percent discount ..." Keep these cards with you and offer them to people you meet when the conversation turns to your restaurant. I offer these to the cashier and or person behind me in the line who wonders why I am purchasing 65 pounds of strawberries or to the person I meet at the copy shop who asks about the stack of menus I am printing. Don't waste a conversation about your restaurant. Make sure the person you are speaking with has the means and an incentive to follow up and actually visit your place.

An odd but effective guerilla marketing technique that I have played with involves making many smallish donations to your local public radio or public television station. Donations made during pledge drives are typically acknowledged on air, so you want to make the donation in the name of your restaurant only. The interesting thing is that donations are acknowledged irrespective of their size. So, by making a number of small donations, each during a strategic time such as morning or afternoon drive time, you can leverage excellent, and positive, exposure from a relatively modest expenditure.

SOME NOT-SO-GOOD IDEAS
Numerous marketing guides suggest capturing your customers' emails and emailing them specials or promotions. I think this is generally a bad idea for several reasons. Most people are reticent to divulge their email to anyone who would use it for commercial bulk mail purposes. Can you blame them? Most of us struggle to keep up with relevant, non-commercial email and the last thing we need is more advertising in our inbox. Most of the techniques for gathering customer's email such as a "free" Wi-Fi network that requires that the customer divulge their email to create an account, or some sort of contest that requires an email address, seem

unpleasant, unfriendly, and more than a little duplicitous to me – which is not the feeling I want to leave my customers with.

Search engine optimization (SEO) is the technique of rearranging verbiage, page descriptions, meta tags, and similar on your website such that, using a particular search term, it will appear before other similar web pages in your search results. No doubt there are businesses for which this can be important (for instance, purely web-based enterprises whose customers primarily find them through web searches). Restaurants are not such businesses. Few people, I believe, select a restaurant by using search terms such as "best steaks in Omaha." Of those that do, whether your restaurant comes up first, second, or third in the search is likely of little consequence. Today's online restaurant searches are more likely in the context of Yelp or similar crowd-sourced review sites, and proximity to the prospective diner, price point, and average rating are far more important factors than order of appearance on a page of search results.

Various service and non-profit entities in the market area of your restaurant will likely rush to present you with sponsorship requests: "Will you sponsor our bowling team?" "Would you like to sponsor our school newspaper?" "Would you be willing to donate gift certificates to our fund-raiser?" While I believe it is important to be a supportive member of the community that supports your restaurant, I think it is also important to be clear that in almost all cases these propositions will not provide a good and measurable return on your advertising dollar for the same reasons that other advertising propositions don't; they may lack relevance for the person viewing the advertising (the majority are not in your trade area), or they are not measurable in terms of response rate, so there is no way to analyze their potential for return on investment. What I recommend instead is that you view them as charitable giving, establish some amount that makes sense to give each year, and consider them that way. If it is a cause that you are comfortable making a contribution to, in an amount you are comfortable with, do it. However, don't consider it advertising.

GROUPON AND SIMILAR DEEP DISCOUNT SITES

Groupon and similar sites peddle deals, deep discounts to their users for goods and services, typically 50 percent off. They also charge a very high service fee, typically of 50 percent of all of the discounted coupons they sell, and eventually send you remaining money. The obvious question is, why would an offer such as this, where the restaurant owner is clearly losing money on every transaction, and having to wait some period of time to receive their percentage of the proceeds, have any appeal?

The sales spiel has been that the people the offer brings through the door are largely people who are new to your business and who will, if your food and value proposition are good, return many times as repeat customers. The allure is in the promise of a rapid and sustainable growth spurt for your business.

From the experience of numerous restaurant owners over a number of years now, I think it is safe to say the verdict is in, and it is resounding. Deep discounts, particularly when accompanied by an additional cost of offering that discount of 50 percent, can be huge money-losers for restaurants in the short term and offer no long-term benefit. One of the problems has been that the person lured in by such a discount often is not interested in your particular restaurant or food concept; they are interested only in harvesting a steal of a deal. The offer is relevant to them in the short term as a way to get a bargain. Their loyalty is not to your restaurant but to the daily deal site. Furthermore, the probability of them having the characteristics that would indicate a high probability of them becoming a regular customer – living or working in your trade area, being a demographic an psychographic match for your concept – is remote. Worse yet, there can be immense collateral damage that can result from a Groupon or similar campaign as there may be extra staffing required for the sudden onslaught of (money-losing to you) customers, and your regular customers may feel displaced and resentful. As well, your staff will likely not be pleased, as it is unlikely that tips will be left in proportion to the undiscounted price of the items ordered.

There may be a few exceptions, but in the case studies I am aware of, using third-party issued deep discount coupons can be an extraordinarily costly mistake.

LOYALTY PROGRAMS

Loyalty programs reward those who are your most frequent customers by offering them a discount or something free. In the past some establishment have used punch cards, for instance punching out a spot with each purchase of a cup of coffee and offering the tenth cup free. The question is whether or not this actually increases patronage by a customer or simply gives them a discount for the same behavior they would have had without the discount. From the consumer's standpoint there is always the question, "Do I want to lug around one more card in my wallet on the chance I'll get a free cup of coffee at some point in the future?"

Various electronically managed programs have now supplanted the old paper punch cards and some are pretty interesting. Most are integrated with your POS system, offer a flexible point system, allowing your customers to accrue points with each visit and to cash them in for either discounts or free food. You have the flexibility to increase points to incentivize patronage during off peak hours or to increase points for the purchase of particular items you wish to promote. Some third-party-administered loyalty programs go well beyond simple rewards and can become a platform for a whole range of digital marketing campaigns.

Among the current big names in third-party enabled loyalty programs are:

- Five Stars (FiveStars.com), which offers a number of highly customizable loyalty programs and allows customers to sign up with only their phone numbers. Five Stars automates certain marketing tasks, texting customers when they have accrued sufficient points to earn a reward on their birthdays, etc.

- Toast (pos.toasttab.com), a popular restaurant POS system, uses the customer's credit card to track points, eliminating the need for the customer to carry an additional card.
- Pirq (pirq.com) is a simple phone-app-based loyalty program that allows customers to download its app, and then by scanning a QR code can receive loyalty points just like a punch card. Pirq also has an interesting "instant offer" feature that sends the customer an offer upon their check in for any add-on items, effectively working to upsell and increase the value of the order.
- Also consider foursquare. With foursquare customers check in at your business and the check-in is communicated to their friends because Foursquare integrates with Facebook and Twitter. You can run promotions and offer discounts or premiums based on the number of a customer's check-ins.

THIRD PARTY RESERVATION SYSTEMS

Open Table (opentable.com) is the best-known online reservation system. For a monthly fee of about $200 per month, which includes equipment rental, and about $1 a diner, customers can quickly search and reserve available seats at your restaurant, without having to engage you directly. SeatMe, a Yelp product, is integrated with Yelp so customers can click through from reviews on Yelp and make a reservation. SeatMe goes far beyond reservations and has utility for restaurants that do not accept reservations, in managing and maximizing their seating capacities. SeatMe generates automatic waitlists, sends SMS confirmations to guests waiting for a table, and allows guests to confirm or cancel reservations via text or email, freeing up staff time.

FOUR-WALLS MARKETING

This marketing tactic refers to promotion that happens within the walls of your restaurant, to customers who are already there. The premise is that it is less expensive to market to an existing customer than to acquire a new one. The goal of four-walls marketing might include upselling provoking repeat business, increasing frequency of visits, and getting guests to recommend your restaurant to others.

The overarching philosophy of four-walls marketing is to use every asset at your disposal – the interior space of your restaurant, everything printed, the walls, in a way that is a means to a marketing end.

The most obvious four-walls technique is offering a variety of new, appealing, well-executed specials that keep the diner engaged. Similarly, revisiting your menu frequently and deleting slower-moving items and replacing them with new features works to increase guest experimentation and interest.

The quality of service that the guest receives can be viewed as a form of in-house marketing.

Appearance, on multiple levels, can be seen as an aspect of four walls marketing. This includes the uniform or attire of the staff, making sure that they are easily recognizable as employees and make a positive contribution to the overall aesthetic. The visual aesthetics, from the art on the walls to the graphic design of the menus all work for or against your goals in your four walls marketing.

Your restaurant's story can be seen as part of this sort of internal marketing. Your story might be about how the restaurant came about, its history, your food philosophy; or the history of the building and works to set your restaurant apart from others and gives it a personality in the minds of your guests. It may be expressed on the back of your menu, through photographs on the wall, or as a wall hanging.

Walls can be utilized for photos of famous guests, reviews, awards, and certifications, all of which advance a marketing end.

UPSELLING

Upselling, that is, selling additional item to the customer through suggestion, is a cornerstone of four-walls marketing. Done poorly, upselling is intrusive and irritating to the customer. Done well, it can assist the customer to have their ideal experience.

One aspect of upselling is suggesting natural pairings. For instance, if a customer orders and egg dish without meat you might ask, "Would you like bacon with sausage with that?" This avenue of upselling is based on the order taker's knowledge of the menu and what would naturally accompany the dish being ordered and therefore, its relevance, and is less likely to be annoying to the customer than the suggestion of unrelated items.

Another common upselling technique is offering a more expensive item than the one the customer ordered. If done abruptly or too forcefully, this can be awkward and off-putting to the customer. A natural way to do this is simply to inform the custom of the other option, almost as though as a side note. For instance, while taking an order for brewed coffee, the server might mention, "Oh, just so you know, we also have a full menu of espresso drinks."

The presentation of specials is an upsell opportunity. It is important that the server has tried the special that day and can accurately describe it.

The best upselling is based on sincerity, the desire to assist the customer in navigating their dining experience so that it is ideal.

YOUR ADVERTISING TOOLBOX

Many very successful restaurants I know of do no paid advertising whatsoever. Other equally successful ones advertise extensively. Rather than thinking of advertising as an overall requisite category of expense, it is helpful to think of it as a toolbox full of tools, each of which can assist you to solve a different problem and each of which will be utterly useless to solve some other problem. Having underutilized capacity for brunch presents one issue that may be cost-effectively addressed through one sort of advertising. Wishing to increase the average ticket size might entail a different approach to advertising. Wanting to steer your customers toward higher-profit margin items is a completely different approach. Effectively advertising your restaurant will take as much creativity, research, and critical thinking as the food part of your restaurant – lots.

Seventeen

Making your restaurant a neighborhood institution

What would you like your restaurant want to mature into? Obviously we all want our restaurants to become well-established, to be profitable, and perhaps to grow and expand to different locations. That is all fine, but in addition to these things, I believe there is pinnacle, a special place that a local independent restaurant can occupy in the hearts and minds of its customers that, despite being an enviable distinction, is seldom discussed and analyzed. What I am talking about is the status of being considered a neighborhood institution.

Some people you meet in life might be agreeable enough but hardly make an impression on you, while with others you may form a deep bond, and were they to suddenly disappear from your life, you would feel a palpable void. Similarly with restaurants, there are many that are perfectly satisfactory in every way, yet still utterly forgettable. Other restaurants through, you develop a fondness for, a bond with, and feel a need to share them with those closest to you. These are the rare places that become regarded as an institution.

When we think of restaurant as an institution, there is generally the elements of longevity and history; the place has been around for a long time. However, longevity does not guarantee a restaurant will be particularly good, well thought of, or in itself confer institutional status. The world is full of restaurants that aren't particularly good, nor adored, but still manage to survive year after year. Nor, I believe, is having been around for decades a prerequisite for a restaurant to be thought of as an institution. Bonds and traditions don't always take long to develop, particularly if the restaurant is purposely cultivating them.

What then makes a restaurant an institution? Is there a strong bond that the community patronizing the restaurant feels toward it? If so, how is that bond demonstrated? Is the restaurant an integral part of the living landscape, an essential component the sense of place that a person feels for a given geographic area? When you think affectionately about a town you used to live in, or a neighborhood in your own town you only occasionally visit, does a certain restaurant always come to mind? Is there a place you take your visiting out-of-town guests and family to show them what the "real" local cuisine is like? Is there one restaurant that would make you feel heartbroken if it were to close its doors?

There may be a strong personal history tied to the restaurant. Maybe you remember fondly going there with your parents, or have enjoyed introducing your kids it or, with a partner, felt it was "your" place.

The restaurants that I think of as neighborhood institutions have a unique ability to draw customers from a variety of classes and races, and becomes itself the common denominator, the unifying experience that brings diverse people together. One undeniable restaurant "institution" in my town is famous for having dining rooms filled with happy patrons that include university students, business people, street people, and local celebrities.

While some restaurants that I know that have achieved institution status are among the most profitable of their type, being thought of as an institution in itself does not guarantee profitability. However, owning a restaurant that is viewed by your customers as an institution, as the place they bring visiting friends and family, as the place that in some way represents their identity, and their emotional sensibilities about food and place, is immensely rewarding in its own right.

So, how do you intentionally create a restaurant with the aim of creating that bond with your customers with the aim of becoming an institution in their eyes and hearts? There are perhaps an endless number of ways to encourage people to connect with your restaurant. Here are some that have worked for me.

STRIKE AN EMOTIONAL CHORD

Food, smell, and emotion are strongly linked. No wonder. Likely we grew up receiving physical nourishment in the form of food from parents and grandparents, those same people giving us emotional nourishment. If your concept includes foods that your customers ate when they were young, maybe at a grandparent's house or with their immediate family, and you are preparing the food in the same manner, with the same smells and tastes, you may awaken some profound emotional associations. In the early days of my first restaurant I would hear the comment, "Wow, this smells just like my grandmother's house" almost on a daily basis.

If you are able to find a way to connect with your customers through a deep, common, experience, and if you can amplify and strengthen the bond by providing very caring and personal service, your restaurant will have the potential to occupy an enviable spot in your customer's hearts and affections.

ENCOURAGE PEOPLE TO LEAVE A PIECE OF THEMSELVES BEHIND

If there is a way that you can encourage customers to claim your restaurant, to make some personal mark on it, in a way that is not just acceptable but welcome?

At Tia Betty's we have always had paper comment cards available for customers. One day an elderly customer specifically asked for a comment card, but we had run out of them. Lacking a card, she wrote her comments on a napkin, leaving behind a very kind note, in a lovely 19th-century cursive, thanking us for the quality of our food. I put the note under a glass tabletop. Some days later, I noticed there as a second note beside it, also offering a few positive words about the restaurant. The practice of leaving behind a note, or a drawing (often a rendition of our logo), on a napkin expressing warmth toward the restaurant caught on and now every tabletop protects dozens of remembrances, notes, and drawings.

Over time I saw that these left-behind expressions helped to create a sense of community and shared experience of the restaurant that was singular to it. To this day I find the love letters one of the most poignant aspects of that restaurant.

PEOPLE LIKE TO SEE PEOPLE WHO LOOK LIKE THEMSELVES

At Tia Betty's, the walls and tabletops are decorated with vintage black-and-white photos taken in our state, New Mexico, mostly from the 1930s and 1940s. New Mexico is culturally and ethnically diverse, historically and now having thriving Hispanic, Native American, African American, and Anglo populations. I sourced photos from the Library of Congress from Depression-era WPA photographers and purchased negatives from the estate of a Belgium photographer who toured our state in the 1940s. I purchased non-professional prints on eBay. What I got for the effort was more than I bargained for. Yes, the walls of the restaurant look like the people of our state, or at least like their parents and grandparents. What has amazed me though have been the handful of times that customers have come up and asked about an image and then explained that, despite it having been taken 50 or 60 years ago, they know the name of and are related to every person in the image! How can you not feel a certain fondness for a restaurant when photos of your ancestors adorn the wall?

LOCAL NOSTALGIA

A generalized, non-specific, nostalgia is a common theme in many restaurants. One sandwich chain features turn-of-the century photos of the city in which the chain started as its wallpaper theme. I think that sort of non-specific historical referencing can be visually interesting but, unless you grew up there, probably does not have much emotional punch. Nostalgia for a specific place is something different, more interesting, and more emotionally engaging.

At one of my restaurants I decorated with 30, 40, and 50-year-old street maps from our city. I was amazed at how often older customers would sit at the tables with these maps and spend the entire meal pointing to spots on the maps and arguing which streets existed when, and exchanging recollections. I have also used black-and-white snapshots of restaurants in our city from the same time periods that no longer exist and with menus from local restaurants of years past. Evoking local nostalgia can be a very sweet and appreciated thing, and is something only a local independent restaurant could pull off authentically.

The techniques will vary, depending on your concept and context, but however you do it, it is well worth giving people a reason to feel emotionally connected to your restaurant. Well-prepared food, good service, and good value are prerequisites, but if you stop at these things, you will never become an institution in the eyes and hearts of your customers.

RESOURCES

Podcast: What it takes to become an institution. Celebrity Dinner Party #18: Restaurateurs Keene and Megan Addington of The Tortoise Club. soundcloud.com/the-dinner-party-1/dp2go-008-tortoise-club

Eighteen

Iterative improvements and growth

Much like any other system that is complex and responsive to a number of different and changing inputs, your restaurant will not be born functioning perfectly. Numerous iterations or cycles of adjustment and change will be required for your restaurant's survival. Your ability to observe areas in which there is potential for improvement, and to make the improvements while still adhering to your core concept, is essential. Continual iterations of review and fine-tuning of all aspects of your operations are necessary and likely one of the best, highest-return, uses of your time.

Growth as well necessitates change. With significant growth comes the need to increase capacity and speed of order taking, production, food delivery, staffing, and seating. My restaurants have experienced average gross annual sales growth rates of between 10 to 30 percent per year, and I think this is not an atypical trajectory for independent restaurants that manage to tap into unmet needs, and that are a good fit for their trade areas.

MENU REVISIONS
Menu revisions other than price changes generally happen in one of two ways: retiring slow-selling items and adding new items. With a POS

system you can monitor per-item sales and identify underperforming ones. Slow-moving items reduce your sales, reduce the overall appeal of your restaurant, and may increase your loss and spoilage rate if they require unique ingredients with a short shelf life.

However, not all slow sellers should be purged automatically. Some fill a structural or balancing function for your menu, perhaps being the only vegan or gluten-free item in their class. In this case, rather than eliminating the item, consider substituting another that fills that same need but is more popular. The fact that an item is vegetarian, vegan, or gluten or lactose-free in no way excuses it being unpopular since, if it is a tasty and compelling dish, it should attract people who don't necessarily have the same dietary restriction.

Before opening my second restaurant, La Waffleria, Wade, my kitchen manager, and I camped out at the restaurant for several weeks developing sauces, testing recipes, refining production techniques. We felt it imperative that we have a vegan waffle, but eliminating eggs, which serve as the primary binder and keep the waffle from disintegrating, was challenging. We settled on a savory chickpea-based falafel waffle that we served with a tahini spread. The waffle proved immensely unpopular. Vegan customers, excited at the prospect of a sweet, fluffy, syrupy breakfast waffle, were crestfallen to see only the decidedly unsweet, dense, green falafel waffle. One would-be customer, a vegan who had stood in line for half an hour to order, literally cried in disappointment. We retreated to the kitchen and came up with a sweet coconut-milk/rice flour waffle that used xanthium gum and apple sauce as the binder. We serve it with a brilliant orange mango puree and a scored and turned-inside-out half mango. The vegan and gluten-free Bombay Coconut waffle, as we christened it, has become one of our top-selling waffle combinations and was the feature waffle in the segment of the Cooking Channel show Cheap Eats that was filmed at La Waffleria.

We learned that menu items developed for vegans, if done well, can have great crossover appeal.

Over time it makes sense to add new items to your menu. This keeps your existing customers engaged and keeps the menu fresh and interesting. However, beware of menu creep, of the tendency of menus to become larger and larger over time. An overly long menu has the potential to increase the number of unique items you must purchase and stock, which can increase spoilage and waste, and be difficult to navigate and off-putting for your customers. By implementing a rule that any addition to the menu must be offset by a deletion of an item in the same class, you will ensure that your overall menu length and the balance between categories remains constant.

KITCHEN REVISIONS

As you become established and grow, so too will the demands placed on your kitchen. It is rare that a restaurant can expand the footprint of its kitchen, so gains in capacity will need to come about through reconfiguring and optimizing the kitchen layout, expanding the type of equipment that is being used most at the expense of the equipment that is used least, replacing more general-use equipment with equipment that is very specialized for the particular task you require.

You can expand some kitchen capacity, particularly refrigeration capacity, by utilizing more vertical space; for instance, replacing chest freezers with tall reach-in freezers and extending shelving to the ceilings.

If the maximum amount of electrical power to your kitchen is a limiting factor, you may investigate the cost of an upgrade to a higher-amperage service. More amperage might allow you to switch some equipment from operating on 110V to operating on 220V, potentially giving you more production capacity with the same equipment footprint.

SPACE REVISIONS

If your restaurant does well, you will likely want to increase seating capacity. If you are leasing space in a multi-tenant retail center, you may be able to take over an adjacent space if it becomes available. Also, you may be able to expand exterior seating areas without great expense. The most expensive option is always to enlarge and increase the footprint of your building. Expanding the footprint of your facility may necessitate other changes, including the number and size of bathrooms and the required parking.

GROWTH AND EXPANSION OPPORTUNITIES

One of the curious things about owning a successful restaurant is that as difficult as it may have been to get your first restaurant off the ground, once it is evident that you have become established and successful, you will likely have abundant offers of real estate for future locations. Commercial property owners are business people, and the ones who are directly involved in managing their property are often on the lookout for a tenant who would do well in one of their properties and who would drive traffic to their retail center.

In the second year of operation of my first restaurant, I began to receive offers from a number of different building owners asking me to open a restaurant in their building or retail center. One even offered free rent for several years on a beautiful and completely built out restaurant, with no commitment on my part beyond that. Although it was tempting, ultimately I declined, as the population density surrounding the property was insufficient to support my concept, even with free rent.

Be very cautious about rapid expansion. Free rent sounds great but may not mean much in the long run if the trade area surrounding the premises does not have the population density and demographics to support your restaurant.

If you decide to expand, one choice you will have is whether to seek to replicate the concept you used for the first store by finding a different trade area with similar demographics, or to develop a completely different concept. There are advantages of each approach.

If your first restaurant is highly successful, you may just want to clone it. If your gross sales per square foot are particularly high, and or if your major expense ratios – your cost of food to gross sales and cost of labor to gross sales – are substantially below industry averages, it may make sense for you to focus on replicating your concept at different locations. In doing so you can leverage both the knowledge you have acquired from the first restaurant and perhaps create economies of scale in your sourcing.

Before doing so, ask yourself if in fact the trade area can reasonably be replicated within the market area you are willing to take on. It may be that your first restaurant did well in a particular context that is unique. Also, ask yourself frankly if the concept for your first restaurant is the best you can do. Though successful, you may have other concepts in you that will be equally or more successful. Perhaps you might find developing unique restaurant concepts more fulfilling than refining and replicating your first one.

By considering a completely different concept, you open yourself up to a very different sort of neighborhood and trade area. This can be a good thing if you prefer to keep your restaurants close to each other, or maybe close to your home.

Nineteen

Managing yourself

MANAGING YOUR TIME

Restaurants have a reputation for being hugely time-consumptive, for demanding long hours every day, and for creating an unbalanced life for owners and managers. To be sure, there are times, particularly in the beginning when you are developing your systems and your staffing and working to become established and profitable, where long hours may be unavoidable.

Many independent restaurant owners view doing the many tasks that enable the daily functioning of the restaurant – managing, cooking, and serving customers – as their chosen work, and decide to spend their time in this way, being on-site most of the time. There is nothing wrong with this. What you will learn by being onsite is invaluable, and it affords you the opportunity to cultivate one-on-one relationships with your customers and employees.

However, if you aspire to develop other restaurants, own additional businesses, or have other significant demands on your time, you might want to consider how to allocate your time in a way that is strategic and leveraged. Much has been written over the years about time management, and most systems advanced are based on achieving greater efficacy by tactically eliminating tasks that offer you no return on your time investment, outsourcing tasks that can be more cost-effectively executed by others, and focusing yourself on the narrow band of tasks that can only be best executed by you. Done well, this system can result in phenomenal increases in your efficiency and effectiveness.

Begin by keeping an accurate log of where your time is currently spent each week. How much time do you spend on writing a weekly staffing schedule, placing advertising, managing social media, substituting for employees missing a shift, meeting with sales reps, taking unsolicited sales calls, etc.?

After logging how you actually spend your time for a week, examine the areas you have spent significant amounts of time in and divide them into these three categories:

1. **Activities that are stealing your time and need to be eliminated immediately**

    This category consists of activities on which you spend time that have so little return on your time investment that you can reasonably eliminate them from your schedule without reassigning them to someone else, with no loss of return. In other words, these are the time sinkholes that need to be eliminated from your schedule.

    A frustration of most restaurant owners, and a potential monumental waste of time, are the number of sales calls that you as a new restaurant owner will receive, without an appointment generally, in person and by phone. These calls undermine your ability to control and prioritize your use of time. As well, they are disruptive. As we age, we become less able to multi-task, and it becomes increasingly imperative to focus on a task without interruption.

    I don't mean to suggest that all unsolicited sales and advertising propositions are worthless, but the vast majority will be irrelevant to your particular situation – if not forever, at least at the particular time the salesperson wishes to present their proposal.

For those offers that are potentially relevant and timely for your restaurant, there are substantially more efficient ways to screen, triage, and further investigate these offers than a phone or face-to-face meeting.

In most cases you can evaluate an offer's potential relevance in a minute or two by reading a summary of its business points. Compare this to squandering a half-hour or so meeting with a sales person and suffering repeated follow-up calls. A request by a salesperson for a meeting about their product or service should be responded to with a polite but firm "no, thank you" accompanied by a sincere expression of interest and request for further information via email or mail, something such as, "I don't have time in my schedule for a meeting, but I am interested in learning more about your loyalty program and I can promise you that if you email it to me I will read it and respond." Occasionally the sales person responds with some version of, "This product is too complex for that," or "there are too many variables," to which I generally offer to respond quickly to any specific questions they wish to email me. Few ever do.

In order to make the best decision when purchasing an item of a high order of complexity, such as a POS system, you should have a broad overview of what the variables and considerations are in the market as a whole and what your needs are before considering the intricacies of any one system. It makes no sense to learn a lot about any one system until you have a good grasp of the big picture. So it is a much better use of your time to do general research and to forestall meeting with a salesperson until you have a pretty good idea of what your particular needs and considerations are.

I do not suggest that you insulate yourself entirely from all salespeople, as you might miss the opportunity to take advantage of say a better loyalty program, or advertising opportunity that could earn a great return for you. As well, it is valuable to be knowledge about relevant industry trends and thinking. And it may be important to maintain a personal relationship with representatives of some of your primary suppliers. The idea is to manage how you acquire this information so as to both make better use of your time and ultimately make better decisions.

Similarly, with telemarketing calls to any of my restaurants, any unsolicited caller asking to speak with the owner is always politely offered my personal email and encouraged to send any information that they wish to convey in that way. If they do, I almost always will review it and respond.

Asking that sales propositions be put in writing reduces the time I would otherwise spend evaluating services and products by about 95 percent. It is a very effective filter on the front end, as less than one in 10 sales people calling on the restaurant, either on the phone or in person, actually follow up with written information. It makes me think that the remaining nine in ten have little confidence in their offer, at least as the offer can be conveyed in writing. Of those that do follow up with written material, in 30 seconds or so I can tell if the item or service being promoted has any potential relevance for us and, if it does contact the sales person and, at that point, having read about and researched the offering and competing similar offerings, ask intelligent, informed, and germane questions, thereby making most efficient use of both mine and the salesperson's time.

By completely removing phone calls and meetings with salespeople that you have not initiated, you can likely recapture one to two hours per day that would be non-productive. You can replace these meetings with a daily review of email, which will likely take five to 10 minutes per day, will make you more systematic in your decision making, and will lead to higher-quality decisions.

2. **Activities that are important but can best be delegated or outsourced**

There is a mathematically simple concept for leveraging a self-employed person's earnings, in cases where the thing that they do for a living consists of many different discrete tasks, many of which can be executed by a person of with less skill.

Here's an example. Suppose, on average, you make $100 per hour and are able to identify that 80 percent of the tasks you spend time one could be completed equally well by an employee making $20 per hour. Potentially you could increase your earnings to $420 per hour by hiring that person to do 80 percent of the tasks while you execute the remaining 20 percent of the tasks. The mathematical equation is: $100 gross earning per hour minus $16 for your employee's 48 minutes (0.8 of an hour) equals $84 per hour remaining for your 12 minutes (0.2 of an hour) or $7 per minute of your time or $420 per hour. So, to increase your hourly earnings, or increase your available time and keep your earnings the same, identify tasks on which you are spending time every week and hire someone else, at a rate that is less per hour than what you make, to execute these tasks.

Whether running a restaurant, or any other business, you have a finite amount of hours to work each year and a finite amount of stamina, so your earnings, either per hour or annually, will be very much dependent on your ability to delegate tasks.

In the beginning you may be the line cook, cashier, dishwasher, and janitor. But, as your restaurant becomes profitable, you can replace these positions with competent people at a pay scale that allows you to leverage your earnings. Of course, this all depends on your restaurant achieving bottom-line profitability.

Restaurant owners who fail to delegate, either because by temperament they are unable to train and entrust others with tasks that should be delegated or because they never achieve the sales volume that gives them the budget to hire employees, will quickly reach a ceiling – a low one – in the profitability of their enterprise.

In some cases it is obvious that a task should be delegated, particularly if it is straightforward and reoccurring. It is more challenging when the task is sporadic, infrequent, or unplanned. Even after fully staffing a restaurant, you may be left with an assortment of odd tasks that do not fit clearly into any one employee's job description. These might include shopping for food and supplies that are from diverse suppliers with whom delivery is not available or in response to an unexpected depletion, inventorying, receiving, making unplanned repairs, etc.

One approach to reducing your time spent on these odd and unplanned jobs is to hire a few people with a very generalized skill set. For example, maybe a prep cook who also happens to have a significant building trades background and can handle most maintenance issues, or a server who is eager and willing to tackle any minor landscaping or organization projects. It makes sense to inventory your employee's non-restaurant skills and see which can take on responsibility for unplanned, or irregular, tasks.

What can you take off your plate by cost-effectively outsourcing? Payroll, to be sure, and for not much money. Shop around. There are a wide variety of payroll services available, both brick-and-mortar based or based online, and services can be as comprehensive or as streamlined as you like.

What can be automated? Virtually all accounts payable can be handled online and automated. We work hard to avoid service providers that use old-fashioned mailed invoices to be paid by a check in returned in the mail, rather than some form of electronic payment. For large suppliers we only use those with ACH automatic payment systems. To pay for reoccurring services such as laundering and some advertising, we prefer automated credit card debiting. For small local providers that do not have automated systems at a minimum, we ask that all invoices be emailed, at least eliminating the need to track and manage a paper trail.

3. **Strategic activates you should be engaged in**

There is much you do that only you can do best. Successful local restaurants are not anonymous; they are to a large degree extensions of their owners' personality, sensibilities, and values, so you should never divorce yourself from doing those things that make the restaurant you. Tasks that involve changes to menu, service, and operations should be entirely your domain. As well, nothing can take the place of direct observation. It is best that you have frequent, ongoing, firsthand experience in your restaurant. These observations form the basis for identifying areas in need of improvement, staffing issues, and opportunities for greater efficiency and profitability.

Relationships cannot be outsourced or automated. Open, personal, relationships with your key managers and with all your employees is one of the best uses of your time. Nothing goes further in terms of instilling loyalty than having good "on the ground" intelligence and nipping potential problems before they become full blown.

Your vision, creativity, and drive also cannot be outsourced. Maintaining a constant openness to potential new locations, new concept, or new innovation is likely one of the highest return uses of your time.

UNDERSTANDING AND MAINTAINING YOUR LEVEL OF MOTIVATION

Maintaining your motivation is critical to the success of your restaurant. How many times have you eaten at an established restaurant and thought, "This place used to be so good, but now it has slid terribly downhill." Somewhere along the way the owner's motivation flagged and the customers sense it.

For the restaurant owner the first enemy of motivation is exhaustion. It is difficult to stay excited, fresh, and attentive to your restaurant when you are overworked and sleep-deprived. If you are overtaxed, delegate more as your budget allows it. The quality of most people's decision-making plummets when they are sleep-deprived, so by working long hours and sleeping too little, you may not be doing any favors to yourself or your restaurant.

As well, boredom can have a dampening effect of motivation. If you are dulled by a tedious and repetitive routine, change it up and delegate more.

Beyond the above generalized challenges to maintaining your motivation, it may be worthwhile to explore the origin of your own personal motivations. Each different sort of motivations has potentialities, limitations, and challenges associated with it.

For many people fear can be a dominant motivator. This might be fear of going broke, fear of disappointing customers, or fear of making a bad impression. This is not all bad. Some level of fear can propel us to get done what we need to get done. A more acute, or more urgent, level of fear, however, can lead to poor and irrational decision-making.

Every motivation has a limit as to how far it will propel you. The limit of fear as a motivator is that once you reach a point of assuaging that fear, the motivation to go further, to grow, to create, to innovate, may be missing. For instance, once you make a secure livelihood, or guarantee a certain level of customer satisfaction, or once your restaurant is well-established, you may be left with little to propel you further, to grow, explore, fine-tune, and express your potential. If your primary motivation in opening a restaurant is to champion a certain style of food or diet, once the novelty of your restaurant wears off and things settle into a daily routine, you may find your motivation diminishing. If your motivation is largely to express your good taste or sophisticated eye for design, you may find that again, as things settle into a demanding routine, your motivational reserves may be depleted.

Surveys of top-producing real estate agents reveal those who describe their motivation as "making my clients happy" have substantially higher annual earnings than do those who describe their motivation as "making money." I believe it likely the same in the restaurant business. At some point a motivation to provide a certain level of customer experience because it deeply pleases you to see your customers happy and delighted might propel you further than the motivation for greater profits.

Understanding your motivations will guide you in the growth and expansion of your restaurant. Each of my three restaurants has a completely different and largely unrelated concept. Of the three, one of them, due to the nature of the food concept, and perhaps current trendiness of the concept, has a substantially lower cost-of-labor to gross sales ratios that the others, giving it and enviable bottom-line profit to gross sales ratio. If my motivations were primarily financial, I would likely replicate that restaurant in trade areas similar to the one it is in, and have a chain of very profitable cloned restaurants. Instead, I continue to own and develop restaurants with new and different concepts. Why? I am much more motivated by the creative act and challenge of exploring, researching, and developing different concepts than I am by the prospect of cloning restaurants. I accept my motivation and the greater financial risk that comes with it. Understand what motivates you and let these things guide you.

One critical element to staying motivated, I believe, is being honest with yourself and reasonable as to your capacity for completing tasks that are emotionally uncomfortable or draining. This is personal – some people can make cold calls all day, every day, so even a weak level of motivation will allow them to sustain this activity. For others making a cold call or approaching an acquaintance with a sales pitch is completely uncomfortable and would require a superhuman (or worse yet, desperate) level of motivation to maintain. Most large undertakings involve a variety of tasks, some emotionally comfortable and some emotionally uncomfortable, so you only have to be motivated to do the unpleasant ones a small part of each day, which is sustainable for most people. The biggest secret to staying motivated to provide a top-notch experience for your diners, and a fulfilling and fair work environment for your employees, is to devote the majority of time to taking on projects that are primarily comprised of tasks and interactions that are within your emotional comfort zone and are in themselves fun and fulfilling.

The converse to being worn down by tasks that are emotionally draining is nourishing yourself with tasks that are emotionally fulfilling.

Your continued engagement and motivation are crucial to building and then maintaining a successful restaurant. Don't take your motivation for granted. Take note of it, study it, and when you observe it flagging, figure out what the issue is and take action. Take some time off, restructure your schedule, find a way to make it more fun, or delegate more.

Twenty

Why restaurants fail: Five perspectives

What causes restaurants to fail? This is a critical question, one that you should revisit often and continue to think about throughout your restaurant career. Any restaurant owner should be a student of restaurant failure, if they wish to avoid it.

There is a great deal of variance between the reasons different restaurant experts cite as the primary cause for restaurant failures. There are no lack of claims and confidently purported "top reasons for restaurant failures," but if you scratch the surface, hard data is conspicuously lacking. The majority of restaurant failures are most likely the result of a combination of many different factors. Also, the people most closely involved in the failed restaurant, the owners and managers, may have wildly differing opinions as to the cause of the failure and sometimes very little real insight into it. I take any absolute claims about the causes of restaurant failure with a grain of salt.

One thing is clear, however: the primary causes of restaurant failure are a matter of perspective. Below I have included my thoughts, having studied restaurant failures for years. I have also included "top reasons why restaurants fail" lists from experts from a variety of different backgrounds: a struggling-restaurant reality TV show host, a restaurant consultant and blogger, a restaurant human resources expert, and a restaurant broker. Each see plenty of restaurant failures and, I believe, have different and valuable insights based on their own unique experiences.

DANIEL BOARDMAN'S "SEVEN THINGS THAT WILL DOOM YOUR RESTAURANT"

1. **Having a fuzzy concept**. I once purchased all of the equipment from a medium-sized full-service establishment that had been open about a year before it went under. I asked the former kitchen manager what the core food concept was and he explained that the owners had, other than excluding a few ethnic foods, largely left that up to him, and kitchen managers before and after him, and that during his tenure it had changed several times as the owning partners had injected their own, each radically different, ideas. The restaurant seemed to have some clear, and interesting elements of a concept – the place had an original and interesting look and feel – but there was no clear unifying concept that tied together food, location, market, service, and look. There was nothing that could serve as an overall compass to guide decision-making and to prevent digressions and forays into random culinary pursuits.

   A clearly articulated concept; a unified, well-crafted, refined vision of what the restaurant will serve; how it will operate, look, and feel, is essential. Without it, success, if achieved, will be accidental. A clear concept is the bridge that connects your restaurant to the preferences, wants, needs, and potentials of your trade area. Your concept aligns your decision-making, it gives you a point of reference and a frame work. If your architect gives you a poor building design, no matter how great your contractor is, you will end up with a bad building. So too, if you have a weak concept, no matter how great your and your employees' execution of it, you will end up with a flawed restaurant with little to unite its diverse elements.

Few things doom a restaurant enterprise more certainly than the lack of a clear and well-developed concept.

2. **Offering nothing special.** Recently I was purchasing some refrigeration equipment at an ice cream parlor that was going out of business. The ice cream making equipment they were using was designed to produce a highly aerated, very inexpensive, American-style ice cream. Watching them produce their product from boxed, institutional commercial ice cream bases and assorted low-quality commercial flavoring and coloring agents, it occurred to me that the core around which they had built their business, in fact their only product, was a very low-quality ice cream comparable to the lowest-priced ice cream in any supermarket.

Though not much of an ice cream eater myself, I totally understand, why someone would seek out the occasional gelato, with its greater density, intense burst of flavor, and stunning presentation. But why would someone go out of their way to visit an establishment that offered up fluffy, low-quality ice cream with mundane artificial flavors? As it happens, customers apparently felt the same, and stayed away. This ice cream parlor failed because they offered nothing special.

We've all been to restaurants where nothing – the food, the environment, or service – stood out as being memorable, interesting, or special in any way.

To thrive, particularly in a highly competitive setting, a restaurant must offer an experience that is in carefully designed, thoughtfully crafted, and imbued with caring at every step. As owners, we have the opportunity to create a unique environment, service experience, and memorable food. To default to some low common denominator is to communicate to our patrons a lack of caring, a willingness to accept the mediocre. The thing is, customers don't need us for that. Mediocre is abundantly available and cheap in supermarkets and chain restaurants everywhere. To thrive you must offer something special.

3. **Indulging in magical thinking**. Magical thinking means believing in anything, particularly a causal connection between two events, when there is no evidence of it. In the case of restaurant owners, this can occur in several specific ways that, if unchecked, can lead to disaster.

   Believing that if you open it they will come is magical thinking. Restaurant patrons generally have a wealth of options, are risk-averse, and need a compelling reason to give a new restaurant a try and even more reasons to come back in the future.

   Believing that there are enough potential customers in your trade area to support your business without demographic evidence that 1) either a quantifiable unmet consumer demand exists or that 2) you will be able to capture market share from competitors is magical thinking.

   Believing that people will pay more for your food than a competitor's because it is in some vague way superior may be magical thinking. The market determines what people will pay and about the best you can do is to pay very close attention to it.

   Believing that if you just had some additional increment of capital to spend on advertising your restaurant would suddenly become profitable (as the owner of one failed restaurant told me) is probably magical thinking.

   Believing that you can convert people, that you can induce them into embracing a substantially different way of eating – say all raw, or even vegan – from how they currently eat, by the sheer splendor of your food preparation, is likely magical thinking (I once had a restaurant owner explain to me that the reason that you would never know that his restaurant was strictly vegan until you sat down to order was because he felt he could convert you with the quality of his cooking).

   The restaurant game is risky enough. Don't stack the deck against yourself with magical thinking. Be skeptical, analytical, and questioning of all assumptions – particularly your own.

4. **Being inflexible**. Although it is essential that you develop a clear concept for a new restaurant, because we are fallible, because we often must operate with less-than-complete information, because we learn new things every day, and because all things change, we must be flexible. Developing and running a restaurant, no matter how clear our initial vision for it, is still to a large degree, a constant improvisational dance.

   Maybe you think, given your proximity to a city center, and research you have done, that the bulk of your business will be in prepared heat-up-at-home meals that busy customers will pick up on their way home from work. If that doesn't prove popular and sustainable, are you able to adapt the concept and offer, or instance, boxed-lunch delivery within a small radius? Can you cater nearby corporate events?

   Being clear in your vision does not mean you are not flexible, adaptable, and endlessly creative.

5. **Being stingy**. A spirit of generosity is valuable, maybe even essential. For the customer, some portion of the emotionally nurturing aspect of being a guest, whether at a friend's house or in a restaurant, is being the recipient of generosity. As a restaurant guest, you don't expect your host to be foolish, say to over-portion, or do anything else that would make the establishment unprofitable, but you are delighted by the little something extras: the bread that appears unexpectedly, the super-attentive server, and the owner willing to greet you, maybe even remember your name and spend a few precious moments conversing with you. These are like unexpected gifts and they express a generosity that makes the entire experience warm, memorable, and something you would like to repeat.

   With your employees, a spirit of generosity may mean not negotiating compensation down to the very last penny and paying just a bit more than competing employers and offering benefits as the restaurant becomes able to afford them. It may mean rolling up your sleeves and running food, taking orders, or washing dishes, if that is what your team needs in a pinch. It also means taking a sincere interest in them and their well being and, when earned, being very generous with your praise and acknowledgement.

Being stingy likely will not serve you well in the long-term. Show me a restaurant owner who is stingy with their employees, whether it be in compensation, their time, their goodwill, or their genuine concern, and I will show you a restaurant owner who is vulnerable to someone like me poaching his best employees.

6. **Failing to employ critical thinking.** In the restaurant business there are innumerable ways to spend money, wisely or foolishly, that present themselves daily. Print publications call trying to sell advertising for this special issue, or that promotion. There is a seemingly endless number of salespeople calling to sell you a "must-have" app, or to hawk this or that new restaurant portal website, or to demonstrate a new POS system and express amazement that your restaurant has survived thus far without it.

Beyond the plethora of advertising "opportunities" there are seemingly endless operational decisions: should you buy this piece of equipment or one with more features for several times the price? Should you fix that refrigeration unit again or replace it with another used one, or maybe a new one?

Running a profitable restaurant means successfully navigating a maze of financial choices on a daily basis, and this navigation, to be successful and to result in the best choices, must be done with logic, knowledge, awareness, and abundant common sense.

"Critical thinking is the intellectually disciplined process of actively and skillfully conceptualizing, applying, analyzing, synthesizing, and/or evaluating information gathered from, or generated by, observation, experience, reflection, reasoning, or communication, as a guide to belief and action." From a statement by Michael Scriven and Richard Paul, presented at the

Eighth Annual International Conference on Critical Thinking and Education Reform, 1987.

You use critical thinking to filter out the 95 percent or so of advertising "opportunities" that, by their design, have no relevance to your operation and nearly no potential for earning an attractive and verifiable rate of return on our expenditure.

You use our critical skills when contemplating an equipment purchase. Finance it or pay cash? Assuming you have the cash reserve, you compare the proposed interest rate and compare it to your opportunity cost – that is, what you can make if you put the same money into some other secure investment – and you have a rational framework for decision-making.

Absent applied critical thinking and a relentless intellectual curiosity and diligence, your restaurant risks being sucked under by feckless, ill-considered expenditures.

7. **Out of the frying pan and into the fire decision-making.** There is a phenomenon relating to human decision-making that has been observed and written about by many. I call it "out of the frying pan and into the fire". The idea is that the quality of the decisions that we make is adversely affected by a crisis mentality. We make our worse decisions by far when we are under pressure, particularly so if we are desperate. A series of poor decisions may put us in a difficult situation, for example, a restaurant that is unsustainably hemorrhaging money. In response, and under pressure, we make a radical decision such as "let's expand" or "let's add this or that line of entrées (even though they have nothing to do with our core concept)." Short-sighted decisions made under pressure can be the final nail in a restaurant's coffin.

How do you avoid the "out of the frying pan and into the fire" phenomenon? By knowing that we all share this tendency in our decision-making. By knowing that generally changes made during times of high stress and difficulty should be steady, moderate, and low-risk ones, not radical ones that elevate the stakes.

OTHER PEOPLE'S LISTS OF THE TOP REASONS RESTAURANT FAIL

BRANDON O'DELL'S LIST – A RESTAURANT CONSULTANT'S PERSPECTIVE

Brandon O'Dell is an independent food service consultant, blogger, and owner of O'Dell Restaurant Consulting. His observations about why restaurants falter are some of the best that I have read anywhere. His list includes:

1. **No unique selling point.** "Good or great food and or service is NOT a unique selling point. If you want to offer something truly unique, you need to move past food and service. Yes, you need to have great food and service, but by having great food and service, you are only meeting the minimum expectations of your customers."

    And: "A truly unique selling point isn't the best food or service. It's an emotion you offer to people, whether it be nostalgia, accommodation, sex, or something else. People remember emotions long after they remember food and service. If you make a real, emotional connection with your customers, they will remember how you made them feel for decades to come, long after they forget what they ate and who waited on them. Food and service can support a unique selling point, they just can't **be** a unique selling point."

2. **Too large a menu.** You must resist the pressure from customers to keep certain items on your menu. O'Dell warns, "Large menus create several problems within an operation. These include large menus lacking focus, taking longer to order from, and requiring more inventory, equipment, and personnel. Avoid the deadly siren song of large menus!"

3. **All talent and no brains.** "What most new restaurant owners don't realize is that having good food and service is only one-third

of the battle. The other two-thirds include marketing their restaurant and managing their restaurant."

4. **Poor pricing strategy.** O'Dell makes a compelling argument for using the gross pricing method: pricing by the markup you need to cover the expense of doing business rather than the commonly used budgeted cost percentage method, where an item is priced at some multiplier of the cost of its ingredients.

5. **Lack of marketing skills.** "No matter how great your food is, if no one knows, it won't sell."

6. **Poor negotiating skills.** "Normally, the difference between a vendor giving you a good purchase rate and taking advantage of you is your knowledge of the goods your buying, and what other people are paying for them.

I highly recommend O'Dell's blog, blog.bodellconsulting.com, and in particular his article "The biggest mistakes restaurants make, and why they have a high failure rate," which is available on his blog.

ROBERT IRVINE'S LIST – THE PERSPECTIVE OF SOMEONE WHO HAS SEEN THE INS AND OUTS OF COUNTLESS STRUGGLING RESTAURANTS FIRSTHAND

Chef Robert Irvine, host of the Food Network show *Restaurant Impossible*, has seen dozens, if not hundreds, of deeply struggling restaurants. In an interview he offered his top five reasons restaurants fail:

1. **Inexperience.** "Potential restaurateurs do not realize or appreciate the specific set of demands that come along with owning and running a restaurant. Once realized, it is often way too late."

2. **Bad people management.** "Unlike other businesses, where you may find yourself managing just one group of people with one specific skill set, restaurants have a ton of moving parts requiring a diverse group of people with varying skills sets, talents, and personalities."

3. **Lack of accounting skills.** "So many times on the show, when asked about food cost, labor, and P&Ls (income statements), the owners just look at me dumbfounded."
4. **Spotty customer service.** "The best way to maintain a positive reputation is to ensure flawless customer service and experience."
5. **Sub-par food quality and execution.** "As it is the cornerstone of your entire existence, it seems so simple that the execution of your food would be your top priority, but so often restaurant owners just do not realize that they are serving sub-par fare."

The entire interview is available here: businessinsider.com/why-restaurants-fail-so-often-2014-2.

CARRIE LUXEM'S LIST – FROM A HUMAN RESOURCES PERSPECTIVE

Carrie Luxem is president and CEO of Restaurant HR Group, a restaurant industry consulting group specializing in human resource solutions. Based on her experience, the top reasons that restaurants fail include:

1. **Location, location, location.** Carrie mentions poor visibility, insufficient parking, and limited food traffic as major issues.
2. **People problems.** Lack of training, an hourly vs. salaried employee ratio that is unbalanced, and an unclear workplace culture.
3. **Poor customer experience.** Disengaged staff, a lack of comradery between coworkers, an unclean or disorganized restaurant, unclean bathrooms, etc., and poor food quality.
4. **Trying to be everything to everyone.** Having an overly ambitious menu with too many items and too frequent changes, a lack of uniqueness, being a "Jack of all trades but master of none."
5. **Overspending.** Spending too much before opening on remodels and updates. Failing to closely monitor cash flow, not understanding food costs, not checking payroll growth.

6. **Lack of systems.** Not establishing systems and training employees to use systems in your absence and not outsourcing to third-party professions when advantageous to do so.

You can read Carrie's article here: linkedin.com/pulse/6-reasons-why-restaurants-fail-how-prevent-each-one-carrie-luxem.

ROBIN GAGNON'S LIST – FROM A RESTAURANT BROKER'S PERSPECTIVE

Having brokered the sale of countless restaurants, Robin Gagnon has seen many failing enterprises, and has noticed some commonalities.

1. **Lack of capital.** "Owners put a business together and inevitably over-invest in the build-out without reserving enough money to operate. It can take from 12 to 18 months for your restaurant to produce positive cash flow. Opening without enough cash in the bank to cover basics is a recipe for disaster."
2. **Failure to market.** "Operators open with a "if I build it, they will come" mentality. That doesn't work in any business. You will need to identify your customer, find out how to communicate with them, test marketing channels, and do it some more before a steady base of business is developed."
3. **Absentee ownership.** "When you leave that critical function in someone else's hands, you can expect that no one will ever do it the way you would."
4. **Partnership disputes.** "Best friends, boyfriends and girlfriends, or husbands and wives. It doesn't seem to matter who the partners in the business are, partnership disputes are a leading cause for failure."
5. **Bad food and bad service.** "All I need to do as a restaurant broker is a Google or Yelp search to see what customers are saying before I list the restaurant. When the reviews say, 'I don't like the

food' or 'I can't get the server's attention,' I know I'm listing that restaurant for sale and someone's getting a deal."

Clearly, the ways to fail in being a restaurateur are many, and vary much depending on one's perspective. Most, however, can be mitigated if they are understood and addressed soon enough, intelligently, and thoughtfully.

Made in the USA
Monee, IL
21 July 2022